THE
FRENCH
EDUCATION
SYSTEM

H. D. LEWIS

ST. MARTIN'S PRESS
New York

© H.D. Lewis, 1985
All rights reserved. For information, write:
Scholarly & Reference Division,
St. Martin's Press, Inc., 175 Fifth Avenue, New York, NY 10010
First published in the United States of America in 1985
Printed in Great Britain

Library of Congress Cataloging in Publication Data

Lewis, H.D. (Howard Davies), 1946–
　The French education system.

　Bibliography: p.
　Includes index.
　1. Education—France—History—20th century.
　2. School management and organiztion—France.
　I. Title.
　LA691.8.L48　　1985　　　370'.944　　　85-22247
　ISBN 0-312-30454-4

CONTENTS

TABLES

PREFACE

This book traces the development of the French
education system from the beginning of the Fifth
Republic to the present. I have attempted to
cover all its important aspects from the nursery
school to the various institutions of higher education, including chapters on the teachers and on the
administration of the education service. The book
tries therefore to be reasonably comprehensive.

My sources have been eclectic and mostly in
French, though a good deal of what is contained
here is the outcome of conversations over the years
with a wide range of people usually working within
the French system - too many for me to mention here.
I thank them all for their patience and unfailing
helpfulness.

All quotations in the text that were originally
in French have been translated into English. Any
errors of translation are mine.

INTRODUCTION

The present French political system, the Fifth
Republic, came into existence with its new constitution in October 1958. The seeds of destruction of
the Fourth Republic had been sown in Algeria (then
an integral part of France) in 1954 when the revolt
against French rule began and where in May 1958 the
army fighting the rebels staged a coup d'état. The
politicians of the Fourth Republic had lost control
of events and Charles de Gaulle emerged as the man
most likely to save the country from civil war. De
Gaulle was to rid France of a costly and divisive
war by 1962 but he remained as President until 1969.
The succeeding Presidents Georges Pompidou and
Valéry Giscard d'Estaing continued to be supported
by centre and right-wing parties until the victory
in 1981 of the Socialist François Mitterrand.
    De Gaulle's brusque dismissal of René Coty, the
last President of the Fourth Republic, during the
official ceremony for the exchange of powers at the
Arc de Triomphe in January 1959 symbolised his
determination to break with a Republic that had
brought France little prestige. In contrast to its
predecessor, the Fifth Republic ushered in the
present period of stable government in France as
parliamentary majorities stayed firm. From 1958
France's membership of the Common Market meant a
reversal of the previous policy of protectionism.
The country adapted well and growth was strong - in
the order of five percent a year - until the mid-
seventies when successive oil crises hit an economy
then dependent upon imports for three-quarters of its
energy needs. The eighties have proved in France -
as in other industrialised countries - a more
uncertain economic period.
    If the political and economic spheres have

1

known great changes under the Fifth Republic, this is no less true of the educational sphere. First and foremost a true system of educational provision has been established. Previously there existed a profoundly divided education service. The lycée catered for middle and upper class pupils between the ages of eleven and eighteen and had classes for younger children attached. The primary school catered for the lower socio-economic groups whose brightest children continued (as far as the baccalauréat if they wished) their education in annexes called the cours complémentaires. Gradually the Fifth Republic established the present tripartite system of primary school, collège and lycée.

Equality of opportunity has been the cry and the motivation for change although the various improvements in the system have been inspired as much by economic considerations as by educational ones. The less able pupils have benefited from the attention of the Ministry of Education with, for example, the creation in the sixties of classes (the classes de transition) designed to give them a better chance of being reintegrated in the main stream. Success in this area has been patchy with the Royer law passed in 1971 being widely interpreted as an admission of failure since it allowed disaffected pupils to enter employment before the school leaving age had been attained. But, if France cannot point to conspicuous success in its attempts to better the lot of the less able, it can claim to have made reasonably consistent efforts in this area, efforts which have continued under François Mitterrand.

Meanwhile the French have not forgotten high academic standards. Indeed their school system is still said to be attempting to apply to a majority of pupils those criteria of success originally drawn up for a minority. One sign of this is the endemic procedure of making pupils repeat years.

The following table(1) illustrates the extent of the practice by taking the first and last years of all primary schools as examples.

(%)	1970-1	1980-1	1981-2	1982-3
Yr 1	17.6	13.0	12.9	13.3
Yr 5	15.0	9.9	10.6	10.7

Apart from indicating the prevalence of pupils repeating years, two salient facts can be deduced.

Introduction

First, the percentage repeating years has fallen
during this period (a trend which began at the
outset of the Fifth Republic). Second, the figures
have stabilised in recent years. The whole idea of
pupils staying in the same class for another year is
notionally to improve his chances in the future
since automatic movement into the next year group
would lead almost certainly to failure for those
who have made insufficient progress in their current
year's work. The percentage levels remain
relatively high in the first year of junior school
mainly because that is still seen as the year in
which a pupil must learn to read competently. If he
does not, it is considered that he will effectively
be handicapped. In fact, junior schools do not
confine the teaching of reading to the first-year
classes, but tradition dies hard. The first-year
class used always to be associated with the process
of learning to read and certain expectations are
made of pupils leaving such a class. It is not
therefore easy for teachers of older pupils to
accept that they have a major responsibility for
teaching the basic skill. However, teachers do not
recommend that pupils should repeat the year simply
to avoid doing someone else's work. Their basic
motivation is to help the child himself, to ensure
that the pupil is sufficiently well prepared so
that he may fully benefit from work at a more
demanding level. This is the major motivation for
teachers' recommendations to pupils to repeat a year
in the secondary sector. Certainly it is not a
phenomenon confined to the primary school as the
following table(2) illustrates:

	Collèges			(%)
	Yr 1	Yr 2	Yr 3	Yr 4
1975-6	9.5	6.5	7.0	7.3
1980-1	10.7	12.1	8.2	9.6
1981-2	11.8	13.4	9.1	12.6
1982-3	11.7	14.5	8.7	12.4

Running parallel with the state system of
education, the French private sector caters for some
sixteen per cent of youngsters of school age. It is
overwhelmingly Catholic and it was the Catholic
Church which controlled education in France until
the 1882 law was passed by Jules Ferry. The newly

3

established Republican governments particularly at
the end of the nineteenth century and the beginning
of the twentieth century regarded the state education system as the prime means of winning over
hearts and minds to republicanism. As the state
system was gradually strengthened, so the private
system was gradually weakened: laws were passed
restricting its role and the state spent its money
on its own schools. By the inter-war period the
Catholic Church found itself unable to sustain
private schooling and it was during this period that
parental involvement in the funding of schools
became vital and began the close relationship of
parents' organisations with the private sector.
Limited state funding began again under the Fourth
Republic when grants were given to needy families
opting for private education. But the sector's real
revival came under the Fifth Republic when Michel
Debré, the Prime Minister of the day, passed a law
in December 1959 to establish a system of contracts
between the state and Catholic schools whereby they
would be financed in exchange for limited state
supervision. The Guermeur law improved the lot of
teachers in the private sector by increasing state
grants in 1977.

Such developments were not to the taste of
organisations like CNAL (Comité national d'action
laïque) which interpreted the revival of the private
sector as a threat to the state system and saw no
reason why one particular section of society should
have its schools funded by the taxpayer. Organisations like CNAL are traditionally left-wing and it
was pressures from these which contributed in the
early eighties towards the Socialist manifesto
promise, endorsed by the presidential candidate
François Mitterrand, to make the education system
a 'great public service, unified and secular.' The
powerful parents' association of the private sector
UNAPEL (Union national des associations de parents
d'élèves de l'école libre) began mobilising
opposition to the government's plans for a new
relationship between state and private sector. The
actual proposals fell far short of creating a
unified state system, especially in the eyes of the
CNAL, but the details of the proposals were
irrelevant in what soon was turned into a fight for
freedom itself - or so many of the supporters of the
private sector claimed. The long-dormant Church-
state quarrels of a century before haunted the
negotiations during the first three years of the
Socialist government's period in office. From the

political point of view, the first education minister Alain Savary had chosen a poor issue to pursue since opinion polls showed a majority of the population supported the existence of a private sector. The government received other warnings. In the local elections in March 1983 the Socialists lost political control of Nantes, a city that had taken the government's proposals as the opportunity to withdraw grants from the private schools in its area. Although the government toned down its proposals, opposition was growing apace. Huge marches in support of the private sector were organised throughout France culminating in the one in Paris in June 1984 when about a million people took part. The Cabinet resigned a month later and its proposals for a unified system were dropped by the new Minister of Education Jean-Pierre Chevènement. Clearly the private sector has a long life before it.

NOTES

    1.   Ministère de l'Education Nationale, <u>Repères et références statistiques sur les enseignements et la formation</u>. Edition 1984. p.103.
    2.   Op. cit., p.119.

Chapter 1

NURSERY AND PRIMARY EDUCATION

THE NURSERY SCHOOL (L'Ecole maternelle)

The nursery school has long been an integral part of
the French education system. Originally conceived
to keep the children of the urban working classes
off the streets, for just over a century it has had
as its principal aim the education of children. It
was the Third Republic which systematically developed this 'establishment for early education where
children of both sexes receive together the care
necessary for their physical, moral and intellectual
development'.(1)

The nursery school has received continuous
official backing throughout the twentieth century
with the result that few, if any, countries can
match either the extent of the network of these
schools or the quality of teachers that work in it.
Every commune of 2,000 inhabitants or more must by
law set up a nursery school and there are now about
16,000 of them plus a substantial number of nursery
classes attached to junior schools.

The nursery school has - particularly since the
sixties - become acceptable to all sectors of French
society. Indeed it has become more than just acceptable. By being part and parcel of the educational
scene today it is now regarded as essential. Parental demand for places for their offspring has gradually grown and the Fifth Republic has witnessed such
an increase in demand that by the mid-eighties
virtually all four and five year olds plus ninety
per cent of three year olds attend nursery school as
the table below (1.1) covering mainland France
indicates.

Thus school attendance in France really begins

Table 1.1 (2)

	1960-1	1970-1	1980-1	(%) 1982-3
2 yr olds	9.9	14.9	35.7	32.3
3 yr olds	36.0	15.3	89.0	90.4
4 yr olds	62.6	74.4	100.0	100.0
5 yr olds	91.4	86.3	100.0	100.0
Total 2-5 yr olds	50.0	67.4	81.5	80.4

at four and not six, the official starting age. The
French have come to make use of a nursery school
because it is there. But in addition to this social
impetus, economic and educational factors play their
part in the promotion of the nursery school.
        The working mother can use the nursery school
much in the way it was originally intended (not that
this would normally be her sole reason for its use),
since it will look after children outside normal
school hours. The most extensive service is provided in urban areas where parents can often leave
their children from seven or seven thirty in the
morning until six or seven at night. There is also
the possibility of leaving them on those days when
even primary-school children are free: Wednesdays
and Saturday afternoons. However the periods which
precede and follow normal school hours (and which
can also encompass school holidays) do not normally
have qualified teachers on hand but women employed
by the local authority in a supervisory capacity.
Children of two, three and four years of age would
strike many in Britain as rather young to be away
from home for what might well be a very large part
of the week. Justification for this childminding
element of the nursery school (which may also be
available in some primary schools) is always
provided by recourse to educational arguments.
Nursery school has for many years been regarded as
a preparation for primary school. It is run by
teachers who are fully qualified to teach in the
nursery or primary sector. It is partly this
insistence upon the quality of teachers that has won
over middle-class parents to the system and one
attempt to introduce less qualified personnel into
the nursery school in the mid-seventies met with
fierce opposition. As one observer of the French
pre-school scene shrewdly remarked: 'Only in France

could it be insisted that full academic qualifications are needed to work with two-year-olds.'(3)
    Considerable faith is thus invested in nursery
schools to prepare children for a good start in the
primary school and, since it has been increasingly
recognised that upon such a start might rest much
of a pupil's educational future, few parents feel
inclined to wait until their child is six before
sending him to school. The fact is, however, the
element which governs the pupil's chances in the
school system above all others is the social class
to which he belongs. Of course home background has
been found to be the major factor influencing
success at school in all comparable countries. In
Britain statistics analysed by the Department of
Education and Science often emphasise that a child's
home background is the main reason which explains
differences in the levels of examination success
recorded in different local authority areas.(4) The
French nursery school seems not to have altered to
any great extent the fact that the lower the social
group the greater the chances of failure.
    The role of the French nursery school has
evolved gradually over the years and is now regarded
as having three major aspects. Firstly, it provides
an education designed specifically for children
between two and six years of age. Secondly, it prepares them to be more receptive to the years of
compulsory education from six on. Thirdly, it
continues its very earliest, eighteenth-century,
objective of providing protection and supervision
for young children. Although it is much less
concerned nowadays of course with keeping luckless
working-class infants away from the many dangers to
be found on the streets, there does still survive
officially the idea of the state supervising its
future citizens.(5)
    The wide-ranging education provided in nursery
school is considered to foster the children's development in the emotional, physical, artistic, language
and cognitive fields and teachers in this sector
have greater freedom than in any other to organise
the curriculum as they see fit. This is because of
the considerable diversity in each individual's
development and the great difficulty in laying down
hard and fast rules which can be applied to the
education of children in a particular year group in
nursery school. In order to further the child's
emotional development a teacher will engineer
occasions for the whole class to enjoy something
together. These large-group activities organised

around a story, a piece of music or an outing are regarded as important for the socialising of pupils. The keeping of animals is encouraged in school so that children may for example learn of the animal's dependence upon them and in order to understand that an animal should not be made to suffer. Just how successful any school can be in the tutoring of the emotions is a moot point and no departmental circular goes into much detail on the matter of socialising the French, perhaps because the evidence supplied by a nation of supposed individualists (by which some unkind commentators often mean egocentrics) would tend to highlight the relative lack of success of this aspect of a school's work. Nevertheless, despite the fact that this sort of education is difficult, the school can hardly ignore it and the nursery school appears to do as much in the affective domain as can be expected.

We step upon firmer ground with the other aspects of the curriculum. As regards physical development, the nursery-school child is largely given a free rein in the youngest section. The teacher simply organises the pupil's school environment and intervenes when guidance is needed. Between the ages of four and six (the nursery school's middle section) the pupils' activities are more often coordinated so that the children play with each other. This is made easier perhaps since the world of make-believe begins to come into its own. Children's physical development is also encouraged by the various artistic activities such as tearing paper, glueing and manipulating ever-smaller objects. The French nursery school considers a child's voice as an important part of his development and thus promotes choral chanting and singing. By the time the child leaves he might well have been introduced to the solfa scale and rudimentary musical notation.

The prime purposes of art work in nursery schools are to give a child confidence and to encourage greater motor control so that he can express himself with relative ease. Naturally this type of work aims to promote a child's perception of the world and as wide a variety of media as possible is employed. The ubiquitous sheet of paper covered in bright colours (and the relative absence of pencil drawings) could well be the trademark of nursery education in many countries. But many other kinds of art work are also done: collages of natural or man-made materials, model-making from such materials as cardboard or clay, and so forth.

9

Language development is encouraged by the child
being given opportunities to express himself not
only orally but sometimes also in a written form.
The type of cognitive development which is fostered
by the nursery school depends upon a process of
knowledge acquisition rather than upon the mental
digestion of a list of facts laid down by Paris. It
is well recognised that the child is helped to come
to terms with the world by being involved in it
rather than being told about it. As one Ministerial
circular grandly puts it: 'Knowledge is not enhanced
by the passive acquisition of notions but by action
which operates upon reality.'(6)

Teachers aim to aid pupils' progress by stim-
ulating their natural curiosity. The children are
helped to observe closely and to order their environment by such activities as categorising various
objects according to their colour or shape or by
combinations of characteristics. They gradually
acquire the idea of space and time, and learn to
manipulate symbols by representing their surround-
ings in paintings. Finally they are urged to
achieve greater mastery of the world by the use of
language. Nevertheless all this is instilled primarily through what might loosely be called play.
Dancing and singing for example have an important
role in the life of the child at the nursery school.
This early socialisation of pupils tends to produce
confident, demanding children when they transfer to
primary school and those few children who did not
attend a nursery school are said to be more passive
at the beginning of their compulsory schooling. Not
of course that this passivity lasts for long. The
start at primary school is still regarded (despite
frequent reminders by the Inspectorate that this
should not be so) very much as the beginning of real
school particularly by parents and the harsh reality
of the three Rs then crowds in upon the children.

The major reform of the secondary school system
initiated by the Minister of Education René Haby in
the mid-seventies contained a proposal to merge the
last two years of the nursery school with the first
year of the primary school which, as we have seen,
would have been to recognise a de facto state of
affairs. But the proposal was dropped partly
because the teachers of the nursery schools (and the
Inspectorate attached to them) saw themselves as
something distinct from the primary school. Clearly
attempts to bring these two types of school closer
have to recognise this real feeling of being something apart. Certainly, the nursery school remains

distinct in its relative freedom from government
circulars and instructions.(7) It has developed
largely from internal initiatives rather than
external ones.

The seventies and eighties have not only seen
widespread acceptance by all sections of French
society of nursery schools but also the infusion of
a freer atmosphere. It has led the way for many
primary schools, if not to shed all the more authoritarian aspects associated with its early days, at
least to develop more child-centred techniques. The
French nursery school now relies more heavily upon
such activities as songs, cookery, gardening and
brighter, freer art work than was the case, say,
twenty years ago. Generally parental support has
grown for the way things have developed and there
appears to be less concern than once there was about
children getting insufficient preparation for the
acquisition of language and mathematics. The nursery school has not however been without its critics.

Criticisms
To some extent the nursery school had by the sixties
become a victim of its own success. It had an
international reputation which had rather lulled the
authorities. Dissatisfaction had been growing
within, a dissatisfaction exacerbated in the sixties
by the growth in pupil numbers. The group GEDREM(8)
was formed in 1969 and eventually spoke out publicly
against overcrowding and inadequate accommodation.
Also criticised was the insufficient number of
trained staff and the failure of the nursery school
to attract a representative percentage of the lower
classes. The school was not therefore offering a
good start to those who needed it the most.

This was the first major blow struck against
the nursery schools but criticism of a more fundamental kind was to follow. Research carried out by
Liliane Lurçat, a psychologist belonging to the
CNRS(9) and published in the late seventies(10)
accused the nursery school of insidiously reinforc-
ing the hierarchy based upon the socio-economic
groups from which the children came. Other studies
have confirmed the nursery teachers' tendency to
support more readily those children who least need
it.(11)

None of this has shaken the French public's
faith in the nursery school and it is still widely
believed (and there is research to support it(12))
that the nursery can help at least to reduce the

11

effects on children's educational performance of social disadvantage.

THE PRIMARY SCHOOL (L'école primaire)

The primary school population has gradually declined over the past quarter of a century from some five million in 1960-1 to less than four and a half million in 1982-3. There has been an inevitable fall in the number of schools although two other factors have contributed in a major way to this process. First, rural depopulation and the consequent urban growth and, second, the merging of schools in the same area. One interesting constant in all this has been the proportion of single-class rural schools as the following figures(13) for this type of state school and for all state primary schools indicate.(Table 1.2)

Table 1.2

	1960-1	1970-1	1980-1	1982-3
Primary schools	74,268	55,326	44,848	43,778
Single-class schools	19,010	17,973	11,433	10,778

Thus roughly one in four state primary schools in France has but a single class, proof partly of the realisation by small rural communities that their future depends upon the retention of the local school and of their determination to resist its loss. Proof also of an understanding attitude on the part of the government and its officers.

A child usually begins primary school in the calendar year when he becomes six years of age. His parents have to register him in the June preceding the beginning of the school year in September. Before they can go along to the Headmaster however, the parents must have four documents in their possession: a birth certificate, a medical certificate, a certificate of vaccination and a certificate from the mayor indicating which school the child is to attend. Clearly, officialdom does not stand by and rely on parents and schools to arrange a child's entry into the compulsory years. The vaccinations, for example, are offered not only to

protect individual children but to protect all those
with whom that child will come into contact since
he must have been vaccinated against diphtheria,
tetanus, poliomyelitis and tuberculosis before he
will be admitted to school. Indeed without these
inoculations a child would not have been allowed to
attend a nursery school. The appropriate town hall
officials (in the name of the mayor) or the mayor
himself in small communities oblige parents to go to
them for their certificate which lays down the
school their child is to attend. The local Inspectorate in consultation with the town hall will have
drawn up the catchment areas. Parents can also
choose to send their offspring to a denominational
school and in this latter case they are not so
restricted by catchment areas.

In some matters however the state is more insist-
ent and one such example is that of absenteeism.
Laws are still in force which permit parents
involved in farming or sea fishing to ask for up to
six weeks' absence for their children.(14) Parents
who harvest grapes are also recognised as having the
right to ask for time off for their children.(15)
But these of course are very much the exception
today. If a child is absent without cause the state
punishes where it hurts most. Absence for more than
four half days a month means that the family will
have its various state allowances stopped. Only
itinerants escape this close control. Neither can
parents delay beyond a week when registering a child
with a school after having changed address for
example, otherwise they will be liable to a fine.
The notification of absence to the education
authority by the teacher at the end of each month is
therefore something more than a formality. Indeed
persistent offence by their child renders parents
liable to imprisonment.

There does exist however the possibility of
educating one's children at home provided that the
education authority can be convinced that the children will be adequately taught. Such a child is
however not abandoned by the state but his progress
is obligatorily checked at the ages of eight, ten
and twelve. Again, if the authorities are not
satisfied the parents are obliged to send the child
to school or suffer the consequences.

If parents are liable to be punished so too are
pupils. As is well known, all forms of corporal
punishment - for whatever reason - are forbidden.
Such strong official disapproval appears to have
made corporal punishment virtually non-existent

nowadays. Other practices such as sending a child
out of the room or handing out lines (or their
equivalent) are also officially frowned upon and
they seem to be rare. The Ministry however seems to
be over-optimistic about the effect of regulations
upon human nature since it also attempts to prevent
the teacher from expressing by word or gesture
indifference to or contempt for a pupil.(16) The
difficulty with laying down the law is knowing where
to stop and this latter attempt to regulate in
detail teachers' classroom behaviour really belongs,
as may be guessed, to the realms of pious hope.

The School's Committees
French primary schools have three committees to help
run them, all presided over by the Headmaster and
all meeting at least once a term. The first is the
Conseil des maîtres which is nothing more or less
than a staff meeting, though its minutes must be
sent to the local Inspector. The second is the
Comité des parents or Parents' Committee whose
numbers depend upon the size of the school. The
third is the Conseil d'école or School Committee
which is an amalgamation of the first two but with
the local Inspector and mayor (or his representative
in some cases) invited to attend. These discuss the
usual school matters such as the meals service,
school/home communications, transport, health and so
forth. They attract little attention though they
suffer very often from the sorts of handicaps seen
in a more acute form in the secondary sector and
which will be dealt with in more detail in the
following chapter.
     The School Committee therefore discusses the
general welfare of the pupils, though very often
specific matters are dealt with by official regulation. For example, the Ministry lays down precise
instructions about the length of time a child has to
be excluded from school if he has certain illnesses.
Thus, a pupil with ringworm cannot return without a
medical certificate stating that he is no longer
infectious; or a child with whooping cough must
leave school for thirty days dating from the first
coughing attack.
     Teachers' actions upon children is likewise
limited. As we have seen, corporal punishment is
taboo but so too is punishment for poor work.
Neither may children be sent to stand outside the
classroom, given unpleasant jobs as punishment, nor
given lines or made to conjugate verbs. Perhaps not

quite in the same league (though this depends upon one's point of view) is the setting of homework for primary school. Officially homework has had no part in the education of young children since 1956.(17) This has been reaffirmed and has been expressly forbidden in several Ministry circulars sent out during the Fifth Republic. However, of all the various activities officially frowned upon, homework is the one most widely observed in the breach.(18) In reality, parents themselves are often the ones who insist that it be given. The fear that their child would be the one to suffer often prompts them not only to demand homework for their children but also to demand the facilities for their children to stay on at school to do it despite the fact that since 1969(19) the pupils are officially at school for only twenty-seven hours. Primary schools, especially in urban areas, offer a supervisory service like that in nursery schools with the consequence that it is possible that some children, by being at school from eight in the morning till six at night, might be doing a forty-five hour week - something that most parents no longer do.

Year Group Divisions
The primary school, apart from the small ones in rural areas, is divided into three sections, each familiarly known by its initials: the CP (Cours préparatoire) lasting a year, the CE1 and CE2 (Cours élémentaire) lasting a year each and the CM1 and CM2 (Cours moyen) also lasting a year each.

The major concern in the CP is teaching children to read. The oral foundations (particularly the letter sounds) are laid at the nursery school. Indeed the emphasis is on the fundamental 3Rs and short shrift is usually given to the freer activities of the nursery school such as dancing and role play. As has been mentioned earlier, to many pupils, parents and teachers the CP is not only the beginning of compulsory education but of 'real' school as well. The tradition of the CP tended to support that view with sometimes frenetic efforts by the so-called 'good' teachers to get their pupils to read by Christmas. Such reassuring yardsticks are not easy to set aside but much re-thinking has been done in recent years about the best way for young children to learn. Thus the CP has gradually lost its intellectually biased tone as various items have been removed from the first-year syllabuses and greater importance has been placed upon such things as learning by doing.

The middle years of the primary school usually excite little interest in parents since the children appear to be simply continuing with a process whose novelty value disappeared with the CP. Moreover secondary education is far off; it is only in the final year or two that parental anxiety about the state of preparedness of the children comes to the fore. It is of course difficult to characterise precisely children at a specific age but many teachers view the period spent in the CE1 and CE2 as a time of consolidation and development of basic skills. The pupil is thought to be turning away from an interest in himself and towards an interest in others. He is in other words developing his own personality, learning to manipulate his environment and becoming a more social being. He is thus able to work cooperatively. The national syllabuses keep pupils more or less on the straight and narrow in language and mathematics, though greater latitude is allowed in other subjects.

The most salient characteristic of the CM1 and CM2 often appears to be guilt. By this stage primary school children should be capable of doing everything that the state has laid down. If pupils are not, it is in the CM1 and CM2 that the deficiencies show up most clearly against the looming shape of the secondary school.

The syllabuses laid down by the Ministry of Education clearly exercise a considerable influence throughout primary school. Headmasters and teachers are relatively restricted in their curricular initiatives since the state sees fit, as in many other countries, to outline national guidelines for all schools. It is instructive to examine in some detail the content of one set of directives issued by the Ministry in order to gain some insight into how the curriculum is formed in French schools and more particularly the nature of the influence exercised by the Ministry of Education.

The teaching of language
An interesting example of ministerial instructions (written by the upper echelons of the Inspectorate) are those concerning the teaching of French in the primary school (to which are devoted nine hours per week).(20)

The forty-page circular begins by outlining the

reasons for the need to issue new instructions: the raising of the school-leaving age and how this has lessened pressure on primary schools to cover all aspects of the teaching of French; the change in the cultural climate, in particular the good and bad influence of the media; the development of ideas on teaching based partly on the considerable body of research.

Besides emphasising the age-old concern with teaching children to read and write, the circular points out that the pupil should also be taught to express himself orally. It counters what are too often considered the diametrically opposed arguments of creativity and rigour by advocating that the teacher balances both elements. It recognises that teachers are less able to cope adequately with encouraging spontaneity in a pupil and recommends that new elements of language should not be forced prematurely upon a child. On the other hand, it is no use confusing spontaneity with freedom: 'people misunderstand liberty if, in an effort to foster it, they fail to provide the child with the means to exercise it. Ignorance has nothing to do with originality and it is not liberating.'

Before going on to deal with various aspects of teaching French the circular makes a plea for the subject to be seen as a whole and not to be taught as a collection of discrete elements. But it also warns against allowing such a view preventing a teacher from ensuring he teaches in a structured way.

The first section under the general title 'Communication Activities' deals with the teaching of the spoken language. It urges the teacher to engage in true dialogue and reminds him that he should not be the only one to ask questions. It should be a deliberate policy to encourage the child to speak out clearly and precisely and without slang. The circular also proposes that such a policy should discourage gesticulation - no doubt with the aim of concentrating the child's mind on his spoken (rather than body) language - though in the French context this seems a somewhat hopeful injunction. Class discussion and the short talk by a pupil in front of his classmates (perhaps after finishing a project) are supported as is the use of such equipment as the tape recorder, projector, radio or television in order to stimulate this kind of work. When the circular moves on to the teaching of reading, it supposes that the variety of pupil competence will be catered for by the creation of

17

ability groups, at least when the children are first
introduced to reading. It then deals briefly with
the two traditional and (in the past) often opposing
methods that have reigned in France for many years:
the one which began by teaching children the individual letters and then built up words; the other
which taught children whole words and later broke
them down. Reading aloud still plays its part in
the acquisition of the skill, though primary schools
no longer exhaustively study a single text ad
nauseam in an effort to indicate all its finer
points. The teacher is reminded that the aim of the
teaching of reading is to allow the pupil to read
silently. However, the ability of a pupil to
decipher a written text does not mean that he has
finished learning to read.

By the third year of the primary school the
accent is placed more upon inculcating a desire to
read rather than the simple mechanics which have
received most attention thus far in the school and
the circular sees this as the time to emphasise
systematic exercises aimed at tackling any difficulty a child might be having. Class libraries are
also recommended, as they have been for a very long
time, with the selection of books for them being
aided by research which has indicated children's
preference for humour and stories 'in which friend-
ship, fellow-feeling, generosity, comradeship play a
large part.' Further motivation for pupils to read
can be provided by the class making its own newspaper or by the teacher reading episodes from a long
story once a week.

The teaching of print script in the first year
of school is optional with teachers being urged to
pass on as soon as possible to ligaturing. Specific
handwriting exercises should be undertaken in the
first two years and special attention paid to handwriting thereafter by making fair copies from time
to time.

Writing in the wider sense is learnt, the
circular asserts, by frequent practice. It is this
very frequency which helps combat the child's
reluctance and uncertainty. Teachers need to direct
their pupils less and look closely at their work
since it often contains at least the beginnings of
something original. Children should themselves be
encouraged to look critically at their work.
Motivation is all-important; children work less
enthusiastically on subjects supplied by the teacher.
The circular also urges that children be allowed to
produce some written work on a subject of their own

choosing when they wish - for example when the
pupils are working on their diaries. Various
opportunities for writing are mentioned. The best
way of correcting a piece of written work is to
start from the child's version, although model
essays can be used with discretion.

The following section of the circular deals
with specific elements of the teaching of the French
language. Vocabulary should be learnt via a child's
interest in a word and the word should be dealt with
in its context. This effectively dismisses the
learning of lists of words unchosen by the pupil.
However, as the pupil gets older so his attention
should be drawn ever more systematically to individual words. They should be shown how to use an
appropriate dictionary as soon as possible.

Spelling should be specifically taught
especially by the sensible use of dictation.
Grammar, at least under that title, is not recommended for the first year but a start might be
provided by introducing specific references to
punctuation and to such terms as masculine, feminine,
singular, plural, subject and verb when the
opportunity arises. Grammar as such should not be
divorced from pupils' work since experience has
shown that by doing so the pupils do not achieve
understanding. Children need to be involved in
their learning - perhaps orally - and not just
given rules. Nevertheless grammar exercises, used
judiciously, are useful. In the second year pupils
should know the following tenses: present, perfect,
future; in year three they should know the preceding
tenses plus the imperfect, the imperative and the
present and past participles; in the other years
should be added the pluperfect, simple past, past
anterior, conditional, present and past subjunctives
and the passive should at least be introduced.
Before a conclusion written by the then Minister of
Education, the circular ends by strongly supporting
the teaching of poetry and outlining a method for
tackling it with a class.

The above brief summary does not of course do
justice to the Ministry's document but it does give
an idea of the Ministry's role in the establishment
of the curriculum. The circular is not closely
prescriptive but instead outlines principles of
good practice. Teachers are thus supplied with
guidelines based firmly upon experience yet which
are subject to revision in the light of new
developments in thinking on pedagogical practice.
A teacher still retains his freedom of choice about

how he is to teach in the classroom. He may indeed
ignore the guidelines (though he would probably
come under pressure to conform to some extent from
both the Inspectorate at the local level and from
colleagues) or adapt them as he sees fit. Evidence
that teachers make full use of this freedom is to be
found in many circulars. In the one summarised
above, for example, the Inspectorate complains
(albeit in a gentlemanly fashion) about teachers
who have paid insufficient attention to the past
circulars and who have therefore misused dictation
for example. Instructions published as long ago as
1923 had suggested better ways of using this type of
exercise but, the circular laments, 'it is to be
regretted that these moderating instructions were
lost sight of.'

Circulars attempt to achieve something of a
balancing act between prescription and reliance
upon a teacher's professional judgement. A good
(if minor) illustration of this occurs when the
circular is dealing with how to encourage pupils to
express themselves orally: 'It is a matter for the
teacher to decide when to enter into conversation
(preferably at the beginning of the school day),
how frequently to do it and for how long.' There
is plenty of latitude offered to the teacher but
the phrase in brackets nudges him in one direction
at least. Cultural traditions of course show
through. One instance is the assertion that the
type of essay which sets out to argue a case 'can
well be regarded as the crowning glory' of writing
in school. However such cultural underpinning in
the circulars often reinforce what are generally
regarded as their sensible tone and most teachers
are glad to have them - at least for reference.

Political Reactions
It is worthwhile dwelling somewhat longer on these
particular Instructions from the Ministry since they
happen to illustrate well that the education service
does not operate in a vacuum but is subject to both
social and political influences.

The Instructions relating to the teaching of
French in the primary school go back a long way. It
was in 1962 that the Minister of Education,
Christian Fouchet, decided at the instigation of
Jean Capelle - a man with a wide experience of educational administration and at that time a sectional
head within the Ministry of Education - to set up a
committee in order to examine the teaching of French

in primary schools in the light of the then recent
raising of the school-leaving age. The Rouchette
committee working between 1963 and 1965 came to the
conclusion that since all pupils henceforth would
proceed to secondary school, and thus the primary
school would no longer form the sole source of
schooling for the majority of French children, a
good deal of the traditional grammar work could be
cut from the primary school syllabus. Emphasis
should instead be given to oral and written communication and to involving pupils more actively in
their own learning. Despite the fact that Jean
Capelle left the Ministry of Education when it was
reorganised in 1964, the Committee's work was
considered to be sufficiently important that Fouchet
decided that it should be translated into official
Instructions for primary schools.

It was at this point that the Minister was per-
suaded by Fouchet and by Louis Legrand who was Head
of the Teaching Research Department of the Institut
Pédagogique National to try out the Committee's
proposals in a pilot scheme involving selected
Ecoles Normales and primary schools. In 1970,
shortly after the results of this pilot scheme had
been written up, the then Minister of Education
Olivier Guichard asked the poet and member of the
Académie Française, Pierre Emmanuel, to form a
committee to report upon the teaching of French
throughout the education system. Naturally enough
Emmanuel made use of the work already undertaken
by the Rouchette Committee. There seems little
controversial about this train of events but in fact
by the early seventies the proposals to reform
French teaching had stirred up a hornets' nest and
opposing polemics on the subject frequently
appeared in the press.

The most obvious factor which brought about
such conflict was basically the clash of the old and
the new. New ideas on the structure of language and
the best way to teach such structure, informed
especially by the science of linguistics whose
influence had grown during this period, gradually
influenced the Committee's thinking. Such developments were viewed with alarm by those of a more
conservative bent. It is not easy for the English-
speaking world to understand the depth of the belief
by the French that their language is something
precious. Generations of school children have had
planted in their collective consciousness the notion
of the purity of the language and its central role
in their civilisation. To the average French cit-

izen the highest expression of the language is
French literature, the greatest - naturally - in the
world. The fact that those who proposed changing
the Instructions for the teaching of French clearly
had no intention of undermining the language matter-
ed little since many began to think they did. Louis
Legrand quotes one example which appeared in Le
Monde in 1970: 'Grave threats at present menace the
teaching of French and, through this, French language and civilisation. It is an attempt, overt or
covert, intentional or unintentional, to prepare the
way for a cultural revolution, itself a prelude to
widespread subversion.'(21) The public debate had
turned into a shouting match. The controversy had
become political though the divisions were not along
firm political lines. The President, Georges
Pompidou, was said to favour the more conservative
elements whilst his Minister of Education was said
to support (limited) innovation. But the political
aspect of the dispute had a more private and ultimately more important side to it. Large sections of
the Ministry of Education and the primary Inspectorate had viewed with increasing disfavour, first, the
investing of the two committees with the power of
oversight in the matter of the teaching of French
and, second, the opening out of the investigations
to include the IPN and the Ecoles Normales both of
whom promoted vigorously the research into new
methods. Basically, the hierarchy in the education
administration and various establishment politicians
felt that the developments were getting out of hand.
Traditionally the Inspectorate working in the
Ministry of Education and the Ministry officials
had a tight grip on the implementation of national
education policies. The formation of the Rouchette
and Emmanuel committees were not in themselves an
unusual and therefore worrying institutional innovation. Reports on aspects of the education service
could easily be buried if necessary. It was the
involvement of the IPN and the Ecoles Normales and
the piloting of the new ideas which was unique both
in its scale and its independence of the Ministry.
    Two other factors entered the picture and
served to mobilise the more reactionary forces within the French civil service. One was the events of
1968 (dealt with in more detail in the chapter on
higher education) which was viewed by the Ministry
not as a liberalising influence but as an anarchic,
threatening one, the aftermath of which was a
questioning, critical attitude within the service
which was seen as undermining the teaching of the

French language. The influence was clear for
example in the way people now spoke of ministerial
Instructions as guidelines only. The other factor
that tended to strengthen opposition to radical
innovation was that most of the people associated
with the innovations were supporters of the
country's left-wing parties. The bureaucrats in the
Ministry therefore found natural allies in the
centre and right-wing parties that were in government.

The actual Instructions concerning the teaching
of French in primary schools were in fact eventually
drawn up by a small committee within the Ministry
which worked in private. Needless to say, many of
the radical proposals highlighted by the researchers
were toned down or dropped. The in-service provision in support of the new Instructions was carried
out through the channels largely controlled by the
Inspectorate. The Instructions for the teaching of
French which affected the lower secondary sector
which came out in 1977 and those for the upper secondary sector in 1981 were also the product of private committees.

The whole episode shows a mistrust by the
central authorities of local initiative which kicks
over the traces of the established procedures and
this attitude was modified only when the political
masters of the Minstry changed in 1981. Jean
Capelle compares the French system unfavourably with
the British one by quoting the instance of the
Robbins Committee of the early sixties. This committee was given the financial means to investigate
the needs of the higher education sector. Moreover
it was independent of the government in power since
it was set up by a Conservative administration but
its recommendations implemented by a Labour one. In
other words, it was listened to. It would be fanciful however to place the British and French systems
at opposite poles since the French government in its
turn (in the eighties) listened to committees it set
up, for example the one presided over by Louis
Legrand as we shall see in the chapter on the
collège, whilst Britain still awaits the full implementation of the James Report, for example, published in 1972.

Mathematics

After French, mathematics is the single subject with
the greatest number of hours set aside for it in the
primary curriculum: six hours per week. As usual,

Paris indicates what should be taught and at what level. Thus in the first year it is laid down that children should be taught such things as: how to recognise the features of various objects, categorise and arrange them; comprehend the notion of number and thus use the terms 'as much as' 'more than' 'less than'; associate the number with a collection of objects; study numbers of one or two digits; write and use equal expressions of the type 16=12+4; use the signs for 'is equal to' 'is not equal to' 'is more than' 'is less than'; write out a series of numbers in ascending or descending order; understand special relationships by using such things as squared paper; recognise curves and simple figures; construct simple shapes.

In the first year the only mathematical operation that is taught is addition. Before 1970 teachers were free to introduce the three others. The reduction to addition only was occasioned by a desire to ensure that children had acquired a firm basis upon which to build in subsequent years rather than have assimilated imperfectly a wider range of concepts. Subtraction and multiplication form part of the syllabus of the next two years (in the cours élémentaires) as well as an introduction to division. Decimals are introduced in the final two years (the cours moyens) though it is not considered necessary that this type of number work, especially involving division, should be completed in the primary school but will be continued in the collège. Nevertheless primary schools have a fairly full syllabus to cover before handing over their charges to the secondary system.(22)

The introduction of the so-called modern mathematics in schools during the seventies gave rise to the same sort of fears (among parents especially) that have attended it in other countries - basically whether or not pupils were losing more than they were gaining - though such fears have somewhat abated today along with the obsession with certain novel features such as number bases.(23) Nevertheless there has been a retreat on this front with something of a return by the mid-seventies to a more traditional view of the subject.

The Remainder of the Curriculum

Two-thirds of the time allocated each week to the curriculum (leaving aside PE which is given five hours) are taken up by mathematics and French. The remaining one-third (seven hours) is what is left for all the rest. This part of the curriculum is grouped under the catch-all title of activités d'éveil, activities which are supposed to include what are more familiarly known as history, geography, science, art and craft, music and moral education. The Ministry of Education has occasionally attempted to define exactly what common ground is shared by these disparate disciplines. One official publication declared that the teaching of these activités d'éveil (literally translated as 'awakening activities') had a common purpose: 'The dominant feature of this teaching is that it rests upon the processes by which is progressively developed the personality of each child and upon the need to bring about, to understand, to communicate what is entailed by them.'(24) What could be vaguer? Perhaps little else could be expected from any attempt to define as one family the above list of disciplines. Administrative convenience rather than logical analysis seems to have given rise to this all-embracing category of the curriculum. Nevertheless such categorisation is not without its educational justification.

At the end of the sixties dissatisfaction was growing with the way these various disciplines were being taught, particularly history, geography and science. Each was largely conceived as a separate entity and each had a delimited syllabus which depended very much upon the memorisation of facts. Eventually the idea gained ground that such teaching was unsuitable for children whose view of the world was still holistic. By 1970 the reports of a Commission de rénovation set up to look into the primary curriculum recommended a move away from the emphasis on a certain amount of knowledge to be learnt and advocated instead a curriculum which took into account the processes involved in these disciplines. Thus the activités d'éveil were born. At least the new title gave something of a shot in the arm to those areas of the curriculum which had been regarded as of minor importance. Henceforth various circulars and instructions made it plain that, as far as the Ministry was concerned, the whole curriculum should receive its due consideration - and PE and Games would benefit from this reassessment also.

Of course old attitudes among parents (and teachers) die hard and concern is still expressed about the gaps in children's knowledge of, say, two thousand years of French history. Perhaps such concern is fuelled by the general aims of the

activités d'éveil the purpose of which are again
vaguely expressed. They are supposed to develop:
physical and psycho-motor control; sensibility and
emotional balance; socialisation of pupils; method-
ological procedures and mental, notional and
conceptual potential.(25) However, if the teacher
has been allowed greater freedom to interpret
Ministry aims and those aims are vague (perhaps
necessarily so) for pupils at the outset of their
period of compulsory education, the definition of
what is expected of pupils becomes increasingly
explicit as the child progresses through the primary
school. The disciplines become more individual and
therefore recognisable. The Ministry finally
insists upon certain subject-matter having been
taught to children by the time they leave primary
school. Thus to take history as an example,
teachers must have covered: pre-history, pre-Roman
Gaul and the Gallo-Roman period, the High Middle
Ages, the twelfth and thirteenth-century renaissance,
the Ancien Régime, the French Revolution and the
Empire, the changes brought about by the nineteenth
century, the two World Wars and the period since
1945. It might be asked what has been left out and
therefore what is the difference between the history
syllabus now and that enforced before the seventies.
The fact is of course that the actual periods
studied have changed very little. The French
primary school still covers most of the ages that
man has been on the Earth. The difference between
the old and new lies principally in the approach to
them. As was previously stated, the emphasis lies
less upon the assimilation of facts and more upon
the child's involvement in his learning. Nevertheless it is clear that the aim of the history
syllabus is to give the primary school child an
overall picture of the history of France and that
the various landmarks, dates, events and personal-
ities are all to be covered. There is obviously no
attempt to enter into any detail but the child is
expected to gain a historical perspective. There is
here then on the part of the Ministry of Education
and the Inspectorate an attempt at the creation of
some uniformity in the teaching of history. All
French children are expected to have been given
the same opportunity to view human development
chronologically (or, more specifically, the development of the French people). The Inspectorate tries
to strike a balance between prescription and freedom. On the one hand it believes that all French
schoolchildren should cover the same historical

26

periods and this implies that there is something of
a consensus about what these periods should be. On
the other hand, it leaves the teachers relatively
free to teach the syllabus as they will. In reality
however the Inspectorate keeps a close eye on the
teaching since it not only lays down which periods
must be studied but also goes further and disingen-
uously suggests the major features of each period
that the teacher might well look at... Thus, in
the nineteenth century, proposed for study is the
Industrial Revolution, transport, political
changes, French education; for the twentieth
century, up to the present time, the following
themes are suggested: the World Wars and their consequences, France under the Occupation, the Resistance, the development of French society since 1945,
technical progress and the major world influences _
upon contemporary society.(26) Moreover the
Inspectorate - as we have seen in the French syllabus - would suggest methods of putting across
certain ideas. French teachers thus have a reasonably good idea of what is expected of them, though
of course there still remains a relatively large
area for individual interpretation. Just how great
an area the teacher has depends very much upon each
teacher. A reasonably well-defined syllabus can
help teachers plan their work confident in the knowledge that it is the product of a good deal of high-
powered thinking. The danger is of course that
teachers would take such syllabuses not so much as
the official declaration of intent but as tablets of
stone. Thus no matter how often the Inspectorate
states that certain parts of its pronouncements are
offered only as suggestions, some teachers will
cling desperately on to anything emanating from the
Ministry.
There exists then a constant tension within the
French education system. There has always been
sufficient play within what on the surface appears
to be an all powerful bureaucratic machine
controlled from Paris and the reality of the classroom for individual teachers to exercise their
profession more or less as they will. Indeed they
have been aided in their individual interpretation
by the very way that ministerial instructions and
syllabuses have often been scattered throughout the
mass of documentation that pours out from Paris upon
subjects only tenuously related to a classroom
teacher's immediate concerns. In a way this
individual room for manoeuvre appears to accord with
the emphasis by the Socialist government upon de-

centralised decision-making. Socialist Ministers of
Education have accepted the inability of Paris to
impose its will upon a huge body of unconvinced
practitioners. Yet these Ministers still see themselves as offering firm guidance. They have not
adopted a laissez-faire attitude. This is hardly
surprising given the directive tradition of the
Ministry of Education and the long-cherished
Socialist belief in centralised planning.

Thus not only does the individual teacher
derive his freedom from disorganised Instructions
but also from the opposing ideological pulls
exercised upon Ministers. There is no sign of these
tensions abating. We shall see in later chapters
the recent attempts to throw more responsibility
on to the periphery of the system but here we shall
mention one attempt to tighten control. The mid-
eighties are seeing an effort to organise ministerial Instructions better. Thus henceforth the primary curriculum is to be divided into six major
areas: French, mathematics, science and technology,
history, geography (including civics), physical
education and games and finally artistic education.
Not only are the various elements of the syllabuses
to be brought together but the Ministry intends
publishing guidelines on how to teach them. Moreover this rationalisation is to be applied gradually
to the secondary sector as well. No doubt this new
departure will be welcomed by many teachers as
guidelines will help them plan their work. Nevertheless clear parameters for theory and practice
will be set up by the central government the very
clarity of which will make them that much more
difficult to ignore.

NOTES

1. Décret du 18 jan. 1887.
2. Ministère de l'Education Nationale,
Répères et références statistiques sur les enseignements et la formation, (1984) p.97.
3. Alasdair F.B.Roberts, 'Pressures on French
Pre-School Education', Comparative Education Vol.13,
No.3, Oct.1977.
4. See, for example, DES Statistical
Bulletin 13/84.
5. See Circulaire du 2 aout 1977. Préambule.
6. Circulaire du 4 août 1977. La connaissance
de l'environnement.
7. Le Courrier de l'Education, 24 oct. 1977.

8.   Groupe d'études pour la défense et la rénovation de l'école maternelle.

9.   Centre national de recherche scientifique.

10. Une école maternelle (1976) and La Maternelle: une école différente?

11. For example, GEDREM, Echec et maternelle (1980); Institut national de la recherche pédagogique, Etages de la recherche (1982).

12. See Ecole nationale de l'administration, L'Ecole maternelle et l'égalité des chances (1976)

13. Ministère de l'Education Nationale, Repères, p.45. In addition in 1982-3 there were some 7,000 private schools, most run by the Catholic Church.

14. Loi du 16 fév. 1951.

15. Circulaire du 16 juillet 1954.

16. See, for example, arrêté du 26 jan. 1978.

17. Circulaire du 29 déc. 1956.

18. See, for example, 'Tu as fait tes devoirs?' L'Express 1 oct. 1982.

19. Arrêté du 7 août 1969 and circulaire du 2 sept. 1969.

20. Circulaire du 4 déc. 1972. The latest (1985) instructions are more flexible by saying that between eight and ten hours should be devoted to language study.

21. Le Monde 1 déc. 1970 in Louis Legrand Pour une politique démocratique de l'éducation, p.150.

22. See, for example, Contenus de formation à l'école élémentaire: cycle moyen, (CNDP 1982) pp.37-40.

23. See, for example, '12+43=110. En quelle base? Les enfants savent-ils encore compter?' D.Zimmermann(ed.) Questions-réponses sur les cours élémentaires.

24. Contenus: cycle moyen, p.65.

25. Contenus: cycle préparatoire, pp.33-4.

26. Contenus: cycle moyen, p.71.

Chapter 2

THE COLLEGE

The secondary sector had to await the arrival of the
Fifth Republic before there was any fundamental
change in its structure. It had long been felt that
reform was overdue and several attempts during the
post-war period to introduce innovation attest to
this. Put at its simplest, it was felt that the
secondary system was just not turning out the people
sufficiently well educated to take their place in a
modern society. Attempts to reform the system
during the Fourth Republic had usually foundered
upon the organised and vociferous opposition of
various conservative elements in society which
feared that reform meant devaluation of standards.
Not least among these were the various secondary
teachers' organisations themselves. But despite
such opposition, the secondary sector (at least that
part of it which dealt with pupils' compulsory
schooling) has been the one which has altered the
most as it became the focal point of an increasing
governmental desire to bring about a fairer system
for all. This process of democratisation is best
viewed as a development which started at the incept-
ion of the Fifth Republic.
     At the beginning of the Fifth Republic second-
ary education was one in which the demarcation
lines were clearly drawn. At eleven years of age
pupils might do one of three things. They could
stay on at primary school in order to work for their
Primary Studies Certificate (Certificat d'études
primaires) which they took when they were fourteen,
the final year of compulsory schooling. After this
they could leave in order to find a job or they
could go to an apprenticeship training centre
(centre d'apprentissage) in order to train for a
specific job. The other possibility was for them to
take an examination at eleven and thereby go either

30

The Collège

into the cours complémentaire or the lycée. The
cours complémentaire was, as the name suggests, an
extension of the pupil's previous (i.e.primary)
school at which he would work for his school-leaving
certificate, the BEPC (Brevet d'études du premier
cycle).(1) Again this usually meant that the pupil
would leave school at fourteen, though better qualified than those with the Primary Studies Certificate. The lycée was the third type of education
and the only one which offered the real possibility
of continuing one's studies beyond fourteen since
its pupils were supposed to be engaged upon the
route to higher education via the prestigious
baccalauréat, the examination taken at eighteen.
Theoretically there existed the possibility of
transferring to a lycée with the BEPC but very few
did.

The Berthoin Reforms
The reform of the secondary sector began quietly
almost at the very outset of the Fifth Republic
with the Berthoin reforms. These decreed that all
pupils would transfer to a true secondary system
and that no one should be left behind at primary
school. Thus the examination for eleven-year-olds
was abolished and a form of continuous assessment
used to determine the best course for a pupil. Each
département had a commission set up to oversee pupil
transfers.
     The idea of secondary education for all was
explained in the preamble to the Berthoin decrees.
The most immediate reason for their being passed in
January 1959 appeared to be the population explosion.
The birth rate had leapt in the post war years and
this new generation was flooding the secondary
system in the late fifties. Closely associated
with the increasing numbers was the idea that the
French economy was suffering from the failure of the
education system to adapt. This influx brought out
more clearly than ever the inefficiency of the
wasteful secondary divisions. It was partly for
this reason that the school-leaving age was raised
from fourteen to sixteen. Almost one pupil in
three left school at fourteen and only one in two
remained at school at fifteen.(2) More trained
people were needed and the Berthoin reforms, it was
hoped, would supply them.
     The major innovation of the Berthoin reforms
was the introduction of an observation stage (cycle
d'observation) which was to last two years. The

pupils' progress was to be monitored in order to
determine which type of education he should pursue
at thirteen. In order to achieve this all pupils
were to move from the primary school and go either
into a lycée or a CEG (Collège d'enseignement
général). The CEG was not a new establishment but
rather a re-named cours complémentaire, and in fact
it retained its close connections with the primary
school. Indeed it often formed an annex to a primary school and, like the cours complémentaire
before, it was largely staffed by primary school
teachers. It can be seen that the Berthoin decrees
were to be limited in the amount of real change
that they effected.

The observation stage was designed to make
secondary education more efficient by guiding the
most suitable pupils towards courses which would be
of most benefit to them. In fact however the theory
and the practice of the reform were contradictory
and thereby self-defeating. On the one hand it
refused to see a large proportion of the school
population idle its time away trapped in the primary
school till fourteen years of age, yet on the other
hand it did not extend choice very much beyond the
elite that had had a real option previously. What
happened was that the strict tripartite division
of the Fourth Republic became the strict binary division of the Fifth Republic. The theory of extending choice by delaying the categorisation of pupils
for a further two years never achieved practical
reality because the curriculum and the social
intake of the CEG and lycée differed markedly. The
Berthoin reforms called for the curricula of the
two types of school to be brought closely together
but in reality everything militated against it.
The traditions of the two types of school were too
different to be made one by a vague wave of a ministerial wand. Indeed the reforms were also contradictory in their attempts to effect change since
article seven of the new law called for the two
types of school to remain faithful to their
origins. Even within the lycée after one term
pupils were divided between classical (where they
started Latin) and modern studies. It was not
difficult to foresee therefore that the numbers who
would be able to transfer from the CEG to the lycée
to study for the baccalauréat would be few; and so
it proved.

Any hope that the reforms would lead to a
better social mix because all pupils proceeded to
the secondary sector was quickly disabused. The

children from the higher social categories dominated the lycées just as they had done in the past. Part of the reason for this was of course that those sections of society which had felt closer socially to the primary school than the academically orientated lycée tended to transfer their trust to the CEG. Moreover this type of school more closely matched the lower parental aspirations by providing some vocational training.

It should be noted that in fact there was no sudden transfer of pupils from the primary to the secondary sector after the passing of the Berthoin reforms. Indeed in 1961-2 there were twice as many pupils still staying on there than had started secondary school. It was not until as late as 1967-8 that a majority of pupils stepped over the divide.(3) In one respect the reforms could even be accused of being regressive. The school-leaving age had been raised but Article 31 had provided for some pupils to finish their education in industrial or commercial concerns. Because this article was rather vaguely worded it allowed those who had opted for work experience at thirteen to avoid staying on at school till they were fourteen. When Berthoin explained his reforms publicly his very tone was circumspect.(4) He was only too aware of the opposition that any reform was likely to arouse. For example, the announcement about the raising of the school-leaving age was quickly followed by the near disclaimer that 'this measure is in our eyes very far from being essential'. The definite trend, he assured his readers, was for more and more young people to stay on at school so that by the time the law was first to be applied most pupils would be continuing their studies of their own volition. In fact, the Berthoin reforms were not boldly innovative but were based upon earlier ones tentatively and unsuccessfully put forward in 1955. Nevertheless Berthoin took advantage of an exceptional political situation to ensure their introduction on this occasion. They were introduced at the outset of the new republic when de Gaulle held all the reins of power since the new parliament had yet to be elected. The only debate that took place on the reforms was within the Cabinet. By the time parliament came to sit, the Berthoin reforms were a fait accompli.

The Berthoin reforms can certainly be classified as timid but in the context of the author's intentions, the social realities of the time and the future developments in the secondary sector this

timidity is both explicable and excusable.
Berthoin's reforms are sometimes vague and contradictory but what they attempt to improve upon is
the efficiency of the school system. This efficiency was not conceived as an advanced exercise in
social justice in the sense that all pupils are
equal or indeed that the secondary school could
offer them equal opportunities. Rather he sought
to give each pupil an education with which he would
feel most at home. He did not envisage large
numbers of pupils continuing their studies to the
baccalauréat for example. Nevertheless the reforms
did attempt to provide some equalisation of opportunity by opening up secondary education to all.
The extent and speed of this change do however show
the basic conservatism of the measures. We have
seen how relatively slowly true secondary education
for all came about and even the raising of the
school leaving age was not supposed to come into
force until 1967(5) (in the event it was postponed
until 1971). Little wonder that Berthoin could
recommend their reforms for their economy. The
hope was that by offering a more suitable education
to more pupils the country would benefit. A high-
ranking inspector working in the Ministry at that
time, André le Gall, viewed the reforms as an opportunity to align more closely the qualifications
gained by school leavers with the needs of the
country. The system was overproducing what was not
needed at the expense of those areas in which there
was a shortage of qualified manpower. The new CEGs
would, for example, help supply the personnel for
the middle grades of administrative posts, a section
then expanding rapidly.(6)
    The timidity of the reforms can also be
explained to some extent by the social climate of
the time. As has already been mentioned, reform of
the secondary sector had been attempted several
times since 1945 but success had been meagre. A
fundamental reorganisation was proposed in 1945 by
the Langevin-Wallon reforms but they had sunk without trace - to be invoked repeatedly especially by
the Left ever since. René Billères, the Education
Minister from 1956 to 1958, had also tried and indeed had proposed just the sort of observation stage
taken up by Berthoin. The wide-ranging opposition
to such a reform had again scuttled the project.
Berthoin was therefore obliged to tread carefully.
He had the advantage of being the Education
Minister at the outset of a new republic and of
having the political power of de Gaulle behind him.

The Collège

Moreover France's attention was very much absorbed by the dangerous political situation in Algeria - the principal cause of de Gaulle's return to power. It might be argued however that in these circumstances Berthoin had the ideal opportunity to bring in something more radical, but it must be remembered that much of the opposition to change came from the teachers in the secondary sector. In addition Berthoin was a man of the Fourth Republic (he was in fact that republic's last Education Minister) and de Gaulle was not noted for his interest in radical educational change.

What the Berthoin reforms did was at least to begin the process of change in the secondary sector. This initial impetus was enough to provide a momentum of reform for the eleven to fifteen age group which has continued unabated.

Gradually the idea of enhancing the opportunities for the least able pupils gained greater strength. Those who had been virtually excluded from the secondary sector altogether because their attainment was not sufficiently high to allow them to leave the primary school were admitted by the creation of what were named transition classes (classes de transition). These were attached to the two types of secondary school with the aim not only of improving the performances of those belonging to them for the sake of their general education, but also with a view to being transferred to a higher class in time. Those who had worked on the Berthoin reforms wanted there to be a minimum of obstacles between the various sections in the first two years of the secondary system.(7) But it was too early for the Ministry to set up the structures to put theory into practice.

The creation of such transition classes, however, tended to reinforce what was still a blatant division in the secondary system since the majority of them were attached to the CEGs. These institutions also ran the majority of the short study courses whilst the lycées monopolised those courses which led to the better qualifications. Not surprisingly, three times as many of the children in the higher social categories went to lycées than went to CEGs. The next step towards a greater social mix and a greater potential choice for those children from the lower social categories was to place all children in one type of school.

The Collège

The CES
Before the creation of one school for all eleven-
year-olds a helpful preceding step was the reorganisation of the Ministry of Education in 1960. We
will deal with these changes in the last chapter
and it is sufficient to note here that this reorganisation helped break down barriers between the
different categories in the secondary sector. The
creation of the new type of school, the CES (Collège
d'enseignement secondaire) took place under the
Minister of Education Christian Fouchet in a decree
dated 3 August 1963. The CES was supposed to cater
for all children aged eleven to fifteen and for the
first time this age group was educated in an institution that was independent of both the primary
school and the lycée. Thus was born a school which
theoretically permitted pupils to have four years'
grace after the age of eleven - called the first
cycle of secondary education - before they had to
make the decisive choice of a future career.
    The attitude of Georges Pompidou, the Prime
Minister at that time who himself had worked as a
teacher and lecturer, revealed what was in the
minds of the government when the CES was created.
In a speech to the National Assembly in 1965 he invoked the democratisation of the system as the principal motive for change. This indeed was the word
used virtually automatically by ministers of all
political persuasions when reform of this sector
was proposed. The exact meaning of the phrase
gradually changed over the years. At this time
Pompidou had in mind the actual physical extension
of the secondary system to all French pupils, the
construction of new schools so that pupils would
have easy physical access to secondary education. A
corollary of this was that all pupils should find
employment so that their education would have been
put to good use. In the sixties the buoyant French
economy seemed to have its natural place alongside
the education system, mopping up its products.
What Pompidou would not have agreed with was the way
the secondary system later developed for, although
he was happy to think that secondary studies had become accessible to all, he was convinced that the
brightest children needed to be taught separately
from the less bright if they were not to be held
back.(8) Thus the classes within the CES were
based upon differences in pupil ability.
    The CES had four sections, two of which pre-
pared pupils to continue to the lycée and two which
led either to vocational courses or to a job at six-

teen. The first two sections (both termed 'long')
were known as the classic and the modern. The
classic was the traditional arts-biased academic
course which included the study of Latin or Greek
(usually the former); the modern leant more towards
the sciences. The two so-called 'short' sections
consisted of a less academic 'modern' course after
which pupils were expected to opt for a vocational
training in a technical institution, and the transitional class which still, it will be remembered,
contained all the pupils with no academic pretensions
at all. The transitional class pupils were still
taught in the hope that after a couple of years
they might move up at least into the 'short' modern
course. If they were unable to do so, they moved
into what were called pre-vocational classes. As
the name implies, these were not true vocational
classes but ones which rather had their sights upon
the world of work.

Rapid change in the structure of French secondary schools followed the ministerial decree of
August 1963. The following table 2.1 (9) showing
the increase in numbers of state collèges makes it
clear that a great deal of building was carried out
in the sixties.

Table 2.1

	1960-1	1970-1	1980-1
Collèges	3372	4017	4751

However, the CEG did not disappear and neither did
the first cycle in the lycées, and it was this
diversity of provision which led to the creation of
the carte scolaire.

The carte scolaire
The distribution of secondary schools in France was
largely a result of historical accident. Within
cities one school might be a stone's throw away from
another and indeed might well be there simply
because of some local initiative by a group or by a
single prosperous benefactor. In the countryside
secondary schools were a lot scarcer, a scarcity
reinforced by the tradition that the primary sector
educated children from poorer backgrounds until they
reached the appropriate school-leaving age. The

uneven distribution of schools made it impossible to
cater for all those pupils who were now entitled to
be brought together in a CES. There was the vague
possibility that most might have been accommodated
if large numbers of pupils could have been boarded.
However this was a solution which would have been
generally unpopular with parents and also with the
Ministry of Education given the high cost of providing such facilities. Fouchet knew full well however
that if all French pupils were to have any chance of
benefiting from the new institutions, easy access
would have to be provided to them. In a ministerial
circular the parallel was drawn with the epoch-
making establishment of primary education for all by
Jules Ferry in the nineteenth century.(10) Education had become a reality for all children at that
time because the state had provided schools within
walking distance. Indeed the basis for calculating
minimum distances for children to travel was to be
the same as that used by Ferry in the nineteenth
century. Children had been expected to go no more
than three kilometres to school and this was taken
to represent a walk of three quarters of an hour or
so. Thus three quarters of an hour became the maximum for a twentieth-century child, though now travelling was to be done by school bus. Children were
therefore provided with transport if they lived over
five kilometres from the school or over three kilometres beyond an urban area in which their school
was situated.
     It was this desire to ensure that all pupils
were within relatively easy reach of their secondary
school that led to the drawing up in 1963 of nationwide school catchment areas (the carte scolaire).
This immense project meant considerable consultation
between those involved at local and national levels
of the education service in order that a survey of
provision and a plan for the building of new schools
to fill the gaps could be carried out. The catchment area for the first cycle was called a sector
and for the second cycle or lycée it was called a
district.
     Various factors influenced the setting up of
such catchment areas and these illustrate how local
conditions imposed their own laws upon planners. No
doubt administrative convenience, particularly from
the point of view of the Ministry in Paris, would
have called for the creation of units based upon
identical criteria, but it was recognised from the
outset that nothing of the sort was possible. One
criterion, for example, was population density but

suitable figures for a sector might well range
between five and ten thousand whilst for a district
it could be anything from 75,000 to 200,000. Topo-
graphy too was clearly bound to be taken into
account just as it had been during the Revolutionary
period when the local administrative areas, the
départements, were created. Even then at a time
when equality was an ideal as important as liberty
and fraternity, it had been recognised that the size
of the départements would have to vary. So too over
a century and a half later would the school catchment areas.

These and various other factors (such as future
needs) were taken into account and there emerged
three broad categories of sector. The largest were
those with the sparsest population. The Ministry of
Education estimated(11) as a rough guide that this
type of sector would have a population of 5-6,000
and a radius of fifteen kilometres. Because of the
low-density population bussing and boarding facilities were envisaged. Moreover this type of catchment
area could only support a CEG of 400 pupils. The
second type would consist of a mixed rural and urban
population of about 10,000 and this would have a CES
of 600 pupils who should not need boarding facilities. The third type of catchment area would be the
urban one of some 10-30,000 inhabitants and this
should support a CES though sometimes it would
include a CEG and/or pupils going for the first
cycle to a lycée. The carte scolaire is administered
nationally from Paris and locally both at the level
of the académie and the département.

The regional and local tiers of administration
of the carte scolaire should not be taken as a sign
that Paris had entered into an equal partnership
with the provinces. The creation of the carte
scolaire was in fact tightly organised from the
centre and was a perfect illustration of centralised
control since final decisions were taken by Paris.
Schools might be altered considerably (or closed) in
order to ensure that the plan worked. It must be
remembered that the origins of the carte scolaire
go back to the early and mid-sixties, the shocks of
1968 were yet to come and the widespread demand for
participation in decision-making during the events
of that year was not yet voiced by many. However
by 1983 a left-wing government was implementing its
promises for greater devolution and it was decided
that the composition of the carte scolaire was
henceforth to be determined locally. The carte
scolaire is tied in closely with the economics and

demography of the area and has been criticised for failing to take into account future shifts in these.(12) It is of course open to many of the criticisms of national manpower planning.

The new building programme obviously affected local authorities. The setting up of a CES could well involve them in more expense than a CEG since they became responsible for between five and ten per cent of building costs and 30 per cent of running costs (excluding the state-paid salaries of the staff). Nevertheless local councillors usually regarded the creation of a CES in their area as a feather in the authority's cap. Rather like the building of swimming pools which seemed to be going on apace, the siting of a CES within the authority was seen as proof of increased status.(13)

Although the creation of the CES by Fouchet had brought about major change in the first cycle of secondary studies, basic flaws remained. Theoretically the chances of transfer to a class more closely suited to a pupil's development had been greatly improved since all courses were now taught under one roof. In reality such transfers were still uncommon. At thirteen a pupil might move up with the help of some extra teaching in mathematics, French and a foreign language but in fact it did not happen. The classic causes for this failure were that curriculum and methods varied too greatly between the types of classes. For example, the two 'modern' courses (the one 'long', the other 'short') contrasted considerably in their syllabuses. Different types of teaching were also advocated by the Ministry for the different types of class. The upper classes were thought to need more conceptual learning and the lower ones were supposed to be more at home with teaching based less upon the abstract and more upon the concrete. Moreover transfer operated more to eliminate unsuitable candidates from the upper classes than to promote those in classes below. This was all more likely to happen because of the way those teachers working in the CES were distributed among the types of class. The graduate teachers who had been specifically trained to teach over the complete range of secondary school pupils up to and beyond the age of eighteen took over the teaching of the upper 'long' classes. These were particularly dominant in those CES that had been formed by the splitting of a lycée and which therefore occupied the same site as the new truncated lycée. The 'short' modern and transition classes were taught by a new corps of secondary teachers specifically trained for the job but who often had their origins in the primary school. Transition classes were taught by primary teachers who had received some retraining. The idea of an academic education being the only suitable one for the brighter classes thus remained strong, taught as they were by people who had gone through that system themselves and who often regarded any attempt to change the content and method of their teaching as tantamount to a lowering of standards.

Nevertheless such modifications were made. The 'long' classical and modern types of class were merged in 1968 with the study of Latin being removed from the first-year curriculum to become an option in the third year. These two classes were henceforth known as Section 1 and Section 11 but remained distinct. The only way these would become compatible would be for their curricula to be the same. This came under Olivier Guichard when the first and second year curriculum was altered (July 1969) and that of the third and fourth year (May 1971).

This was the signal for there to be some adoption by teachers of similar methods across class boundaries and for there to be a more equal distribution of the Section 1 and 11 classes among different types of teachers. Not that this was immediate or total but in general teachers seemed to be lending themselves more readily to a movement that many saw as inevitable. The changes were sufficiently widespread for a ministerial circular to be issued in late 1971(14) reminding teachers that although the curricula were now identical, teaching methods should not be so; nor should it be forgotten that the types of teachers should largely remain within their own type of class.

Before the introduction of the Haby reforms upon which the present system is still largely based, there was one other major attempt to change the secondary sector. Joseph Fontanet became Minister of Education in the new Messmer cabinet under the presidency of Georges Pompidou in July 1972 and from the spring of the following year Fontanet began to sound out opinion with a view to carrying out further reform of the education system. His proposals were to affect several sectors of the education service but only those touching upon the secondary sector concern us here. At the beginning of 1974 he published the proposals which were intended to develop the reforms which had set up the CES.

41

They sought to abolish the different sections in the
CES since they were based upon what was now considered the outmoded division of pupils into those who
could handle the abstract and those who could only
manage the concrete. The consequence of this was to
be a greater mix of abilities in all subjects other
than French, mathematics and a foreign language
which would continue to set their pupils by ability.
A system of small-group teaching would be instituted
to help those who fell behind. It would be possible
in future to repeat only the last year of the CES
(something of a radical break with tradition). Last
among the major proposals for the CES was not a
change but a confirmation that orientation or the
moving of pupils out of the CES into what were considered more suitable (usually vocational) courses
would continue to be put into effect at the end of
the second year. The Fontanet proposals are in fact
of historical interest only since the death of
Pompidou in April effectively put paid to them. A
new French President and a new government had other
ideas; Fontanet's reforms were to re-emerge in a
different form at a later date.

The Haby Reforms

The victory of Valéry Giscard d'Estaing in the presidential elections in the spring of 1974 was to be
of considerable significance for the secondary
sector. Giscard had passed through the academic
echelons of the education system and prided himself
upon being able to view French problems as a whole
and moreover to suggest solutions to them. He was
convinced that socially France was becoming one nation because of the influence of three factors: the
rise in the standard of living, the spread of information and education.(15) Moreover his accession to
France's highest post made him determined to accel-
erate this process and clearly education was therefore to be a major interest of his from the outset.
He did not however believe that all children are
born equal or that school could make them so, but he
did adhere to the idea that those of equal ability
should be given equal opportunity. The man who was
to work out the detail of the Giscardian philosophy,
which in reality was only the continuation of a
movement that had been evident in the secondary
sector for many years, was René Haby. Haby was
eventually to be the architect of the most controversial proposals to be implemented in the secondary
sector during the Fifth Republic. He seemed better

placed than many Ministers of Education to initiate
reform since he had spent most of his life in the
education service. He had taught in primary and
secondary schools, he had worked in the Ministry of
Education and had been the recteur of the académie
of Clermont-Ferrand. He thus came to his post
already having given considerable thought to the
education service and his ideas certainly ran in the
direction of those of Giscard as regards the equality
of opportunity since he had been closely involved in
an administrative capacity with the setting up of
the CES. He immediately set about producing proposals, largely on his own, to cover the whole of the
education service, though the most far-reaching were
the ones which concern us here. Less than a year
later Haby published his blueprint.
    Since these proposals were aimed at changing
various aspects of the whole education system it is
hardly surprising that they were attacked on a broad
front, for example by unions and parents' associations. By the time the proposals were discussed by
the French Cabinet in May some alterations had been
made but despite press reports that, because of the
widespread opposition, they appeared to be on the
verge of being shelved, they were approved and sent
for debate by the National Assembly in June 1975.
It must be remembered that the implementation of the
Haby proposals depended upon any law that might be
passed in 1975 being given practical form in Ministry
circulars and that such fundamental changes that
were suggested would need to be implemented over
several years. Thus the opposition parties were not
any more inclined than the parents and unions to
support the reforms - particularly as it would be
they (or so they thought) who would be obliged to
carry out the law after the general election in
1978. The debate in Parliament was a confused
affair. At one point, for example, the Socialist
Party spokesman, Mexandeau, thought it wrong that
the future educational possibilities for pupils
taking the baccalauréat was still regarded as the
first stage of higher education. The debate was
suspended. When the députés re-assembled the Secretary of State was still not there and an amendment of
Mexandeau's incorporating his point was defeated.
    On July 11 Haby's education law was promulgated.
Its 22 articles are sufficiently full of good intention and couched in such general terms to be qualified
as vague. The aims of the new law were perhaps more
succinctly outlined by a publication from the
Ministry of Education (clearly overseen by Haby

himself) in 1977. It had five main aims for the
education service: to ensure equality of opportunity;
to give a balanced education; to affirm the value of
technical and vocational education; to educate the
future citizen and to make the school a focus for
collaboration.(16)
     Henceforth all children were to receive the
same education in the first cycle of secondary
school, something which Giscard had advocated on
several occasions, for example in his own blueprint
for France: 'The setting up of a single system of
collèges for all French youngsters will constitute
a potent means of acquiring the same culture. It
will have to be accomplished with regard to syllabuses by the defining of a 'common core of knowledge', varying with the times and giving expression
to our particular civilisation'.(17)
     This broadening of the horizons for the less
able continued the general movement evident in this
sector for many years. If this was not a radical
departure, the practical implications were. Haby
intended ending the division between CES, CEG and
the first cycle of the lycées once and for all.
Henceforth every pupil who would normally receive a
secondary education would go to a collège. The
creation of the CES had gone a long way towards
achieving this but variation in provision still
existed. As the law gradually found concrete
expression in the decrees and circulars emanating
from the Ministry of Education, it was realised
that Haby's proposals published in February 1975
remained largely intact for the collège. Perhaps
the most radical change was that all pupils were to
be taught in mixed-ability classes.(18) Again the
logic was impeccable. If the division of pupils
into streamed classes automatically meant the less
able virtually never climbed the slippery slope to
the main part of a school system then ending such
divisions would lead to greater equality of opportunity. This was the reasoning behind the introduction of mixed-ability classes. Nevertheless it
was recognised that not all pupils would be of the
same ability when they arrived at the collège and so
an extra hour per week would be made available in
the three core subjects (French, mathematics and the
modern language). This would enable teachers to
organise classes either to help the backward
(classes de soutien) or to stretch the most able
(classes d'approfondissement). Considerable emphasis was also placed upon cooperation between all the
parties involved in the education of children and

so various committees were instituted which sometimes included parents and pupils. In addition new
subjects were added to the first-year curriculum
and others were redefined. The new subjects were
physical science and manual and technical education
(éducation manuel et technique). Economics and
civics were to receive greater emphasis in history
and geography lessons. Art was to have its subject-
matter extended. These will be further discussed
later but it is worth noting that the introductions
were principally an attempt to make schools more
outward-looking and were therefore envisaged as
modernising the curriculum as well as improving its
overall balance.(19)

     From desultory opposition to the Haby reforms
at the outset, criticism gradually intensified into
antipathy which in turn extended to cover virtually
any suggestion emanating from the Ministry at this
time. The episode concerning suggestions for a new
way of compiling pupil records was a good illustration of this. It was proposed that the bare information contained in the traditional livret scolaire
should be extended so that it would not only record
a pupil's ability and marks but also his personal
qualities and behaviour, any information in fact
that might help explain a pupil's school performance. The fact that the record, (now to be called
the dossier scolaire) might include, for example,
some medical details and family circumstances was
enough to spark off a violent reaction from parents'
associations and the teachers' union the SGEN
(Syndicat Général de l'Education Nationale) among
others as the spectre of the police state was
raised. The original idea that an attempt be made
to go beyond the stereotyped comments usually found
in records and reports was lost as fears mounted
about their confidentiality being breached and even
of their being put on to a government computer for
future use.(20) Various attempts were made to re-
assure the critics that the new dossier scolaire
was being introduced in the pupils' interest(21) and
modifications were made to the original proposal
(for example, the dossier would be destroyed one
year and not five years after a pupil had left
school) but to no avail. Haby's enthusiasm for the
project waned (in any case he claimed that the
original idea had come from the teachers themselves)
and the innovation was eventually dropped altogether.(22)

'Will we see when the schools open in September, M.Haby, hung about with texts and circulars,
setting off alone for the battle, leaving behind him
the troops rooted to the spot with their arms
folded?' So wondered Bruno Frappat in Le Monde(23)
and with some reason. The union SNI-PEGC which had
about 70 per cent of teachers in the collèges as
members had advised them simply not to carry out the
reforms when school started in September. However,
Haby, who had been fighting single-handed (or so it
seemed at times) for his reforms, obtained more
money in order to meet the unions' demands for extra
staff and smaller classes(24) and so in September
1977 the reforms began to come into force.

In fact the Haby reforms were never uniformly
applied. In theory the creation of mixed-ability
classes was a simple matter of dividing the total
first-year entry by 24 (the notional class size)
but in reality it was more difficult. Simply list-
ing a year's intake alphabetically might mean in an
area in which there were many immigrants that half
a class would be arab. Schools could in any case
surreptitiously band or stream their pupils by
putting into one class, for example, all the pupils
who came from a more academically inclined feeder
school. Indeed some headmasters refused point
blank, perhaps because they belonged to SNI, the
teachers' union still hostile to the innovations,
to apply the reform. In any case the reform itself
foresaw the necessity for grouping together the very
weak in what was formerly the classe de transition
and was now to be called the classe allégée.(25)

Even more variable in their application were
the hours of soutien and approfondissement. Some
schools followed the advice of SNI and, because they
regarded the extra time as a way of reintroducing
streaming, kept all the pupils for the supplementary
lessons. Teachers in any case were left very much
on their own as to how they should organise this
aspect of the reforms(26) and some chose to ignore
the weakest in a class, believing them incapable of
improving sufficiently, and chose those who were not
very far behind as the best to come along to soutien.
Sometimes supply teachers were used for such lessons.
Soutien for the less able was at least more within
the teacher's experience than approfondissement for
the more able. To many pushing ahead with the
brightest would only make whole-class teaching more
difficult than it was already. In any case during
the approfondissement class the teacher was not
supposed to introduce new material but exploit that

already covered (but which might have already been well understood). Approfondissement therefore has tended to wither on the vine from the beginning.

Another break with the past that was provided by the reforms was the supply by the state of all text books for pupils in the collège. Text books had long been supplied free of charge in the primary school but it was now thought that equality of opportunity demanded that no pupil should pay for his books throughout the whole period of compulsory schooling. The measure itself received widespread support but its results were often criticised. The new text books specifically produced to coincide with the introduction of the reforms struck many as poor and thin. Two factors explained what helped create this impression. Firstly, the Ministry of Education, the new paymaster in this area, had to budget for the increased national expenditure and so had to place a limit on spending where none had existed before. Secondly, new syllabuses had been brought out with mixed-ability classes very much in mind and these asked for less in the way of content. The new books produced therefore tended to have fewer pages and fewer illustrations with the result that pressure for information would increase on teachers and such resources as the school library. Some doubted however if either teachers or schools were sufficiently well equipped to deal adequately with the latest pressures and the inevitable conclusion was often that the standard of subject teaching would fall.(27) The Ministry of Education did not agree stating that the latest books were better suited to the reforms than the ones in former use.(28)

Largely because of the increasingly bitter quarrelling between the Socialist and Communist Parties, the expected victory of the Left in 1978 did not materialise. The return to power of those centre and right-wing parties supporting Giscard was therefore thought to herald the return of Haby to the Ministry of Education in order to oversee the full implementation of the reforms that bore his name. In fact, however, he was replaced by Christian Beullac. It seems likely that Giscard sought to promote better relations between the Ministry of Education and the unions who had eventually come to speak of Haby only in the bitterest of terms.(29) Beullac was brought in from outside the world of education, having long worked in industry as a top administrator. He sought to do the job for which Giscard had chosen him and

announced on 8 May, to the delight of the unions,
that the dossier scolaire was to be officially
dropped. Nevertheless, he made it plain from the
outset that, since the Haby reforms were the law of
the land, they had to be implemented. However, he
showed himself conciliatory here too by announcing
in his first press conference that some modification
was in order.(30)

Despite the many attempts over the years to
remodel the first cycle of the secondary school
there was still a general feeling that the collège
had not lived up to expectations. There was an
increase in pupils transferring to the private
(Catholic) sector and articles in the press wondered
whether the education system 'had not become a
gigantic machine for the manufacture of dunces'(31)
and produced quotations from teachers convinced
that standards had fallen drastically. One teacher
of French, for example, declared: 'The general level
is falling. Out of five or six first forms only two
can be compared to those of yesterday'.(32)

Although respected and close observers of the
education system were occasionally given the chance
to point out that comparison of the present system
with that of some time ago was difficult since
educational objectives had often changed,(33) there
remained a feeling that there was still room for
improvement.

The Left in Power

The arrival of François Mitterrand in the Elysée
Palace and the subsequent socialist victory in the
general election in 1981 heralded yet more changes
for the collèges. The first left-wing government of
the Fifth Republic intended adhering to its traditions of social concern and interest in schools as a
means of reducing privilege. The new Minister of
Education, Alain Savary, benefited from the initial
policy of increased government expenditure. The
1982 education budget was increased by some seven-
teen per cent and some 34,000 jobs were created
throughout the education service.(34) For once the
teachers' unions and parents' associations found
little to complain of.

Savary, as was by now the tradition with
Ministers of Education, began a new line of attack
on the defects of the system. The freshest initiative was the creation in July 1981 of educational
priority zones (zones d'éducation prioritaire or
ZEP). It had long been recognised of course that if

schools were not dispensing equality of treatment to
all their pupils the fault did not lie solely with
schools themselves and the way they were organised
but with society itself. A school's action upon its
pupils was circumscribed by the quality of its intake and despite efforts by central and local
authorities to ensure parity of treatment for
collèges these often varied considerably. If proof
were needed, it was semi-officially provided in the
year of Savary's appointment by a study in depth of
a dozen collèges.(35) What emerged in particular
from this study was the variety to be found among
the collèges. One school whose pupils went on to
one of the most prestigious lycées in Paris concentrated upon academic excellence. Its catchment area
contained an unusually high proportion of parents
who fell into the higher socio-economic categories
and whose interest in their children's progress
occasionally turned to obsession. It was not a
place for the weak. A few kilometres away in the
industrial suburbs another collège had a catchment
area which had a high proportion of pupils with a
background described by one of its teachers as sub-
proletarian. Parents here exhibited a lack of
interest in education that occasionally turned to
hostility and this was often reflected in the
attitude of their children.
    The creation of the ZEP was therefore an effort
to help change the depressing cycle of failure often
encountered in the less privileged areas of France
and particularly concerned the collèges since what
was happening in them was often the major criterion
for setting up a priority area. One collège, for
example, at Creil (just to the north of Paris) had a
first-year intake of 213 only 87 of whom had not
already had to repeat at least one year because of
lack of progress; one in seven went into pre-vocational classes before reaching the end of their time
at the collège. But ZEP were set up not only
because of the relatively poor performance of school
children. The whole social and economic environment
was examined with the result that the zones tended
to be characterised by underachieving pupils,
absenteeism, rejection of school, violence, under-
privileged families, high unemployment, a high
percentage of immigrants and poor living conditions.
However, the inclusion of specifically non-school
factors indicated that the problems faced by the
education system called for a concerted approach
by various government agencies. This was recognised
as efforts were made to improve the environment in

such areas. Thus, for example, a joint ministerial
programme helped organise spare time activities
for the young bringing together schools and clubs of
various kinds. In the year 1982-3 three hundred and
sixty-three ZEP(36) had been created (both in urban
and rural areas) involving in each zone between
three and thirty per cent of the collèges on the
French mainland (in Corsica 42 per cent of the
collèges were involved).

    The ZEP are remarkable as a cooperative venture
between a variety of government departments and outside organisations. Extra government money has been
allocated to these zones in the belief that although
initiative and hard work should not depend upon
extra cash, that initiative needs to be sustained
and not die away with the enthusiasm of the first
pioneers. But the ZEP are remarkable for something
specifically pedagogical. They were viewed from the
outset as an opportunity to adapt teaching methods
to the local problem in hand. From the beginning
of his first academic year, Savary encouraged (with
money as well as a Ministry circular) projects
which featured experimentation that broke with the
tradition of one teacher to one class in the
collège(37) and which were supposed to lead to
greater cooperation between the various parts of the
education service.

    Since the ZEP can only be viewed as a long-term
project, the success or failure can only be judged
after an extended trial. Perhaps success or failure
are rather inappropriate terms if used absolutely
since there will no doubt be elements of both.
Certainly, given the socialist government's later
policy of financial stringency which followed on its
initial spending spree, funds are less likely to be
forthcoming. Fears have been expressed particularly
by the unions and parents' associations that to
designate a school as less fortunate than others
will do more harm than good. Moreover by depending
upon concerted action by a wide range of organisations the ZEP risks suffering from any one weak link
and from any lack of true cooperation. Nevertheless
the collège (and other parts of the system) is
participating in a new attempt to see its problems
as a whole.

    The ZEP were an admission that despite the
assorted reforms of the secondary system (and of the
primary system) over the years there were still
factors fundamental to pupil progress which had been
left untouched. Moreover public concern over the
efficacy of the collèges as a system for equalising

opportunity was well founded. It became increasingly clear that the Haby reforms were not working.
Indeed, as has already been pointed out, they were
far from being applied on a national scale. The nub
of the difficulty was that logical conclusion of
pure reasoning: mixed-ability teaching. Schools
simply were unable to put it into practice because
teachers did not know how to change their teaching
accordingly. They had been placed in an impossible
position for, although the Haby reforms had been
introduced some two years after the new education
law had been passed, what little in-service that had
been available had not affected the majority of
teachers. The result was that mixed-ability teaching was being carried out patchily(38) and various
ways were being used to circumvent the law. This
was being done mainly by using the choice of foreign
language in the first year to reinstate some form of
streaming. Each successive year saw less mixed-
ability teaching as more options were introduced.
The soutien classes were being less and less frequently used. Three years after the introduction of
the Haby reforms only 30 per cent of classes came
into this category. According to some, the consequences of this confusion was that the proportion of
pupils failing in the collège was reaching record
levels.(39) The Haby law itself had allowed the
continuation of pre-vocational classes into which
the weakest pupils (apart from those in remedial
classes) were transferred from the first form on
(indeed some were already moved there directly from
junior school), so there was never any intention to
introduce mixed-ability teaching which covered the
whole ability range. The Ministry of Education had
come to accept that this aspect of the reforms
could never be applied in the foreseeable future
despite the official policy. Circulars were quietly
issued recognising what was happening and confirming
the status quo.(40)

The Legrand Proposals
It was against this background that at the end of
1981 Savary entrusted an investigation into the ills
of the collège to Louis Legrand, the Professor of
Education at the University of Strasbourg and former
head of the INRP (Institut national de la recherche
pédagogique). His report Pour un collège démocratique: mission d'étude pour l'amélioration du
fonctionnement des collèges was published at the end
of 1982. Unlike the Haby reforms which were largely

the work of one man, the Legrand Report was the
fruit of the labours of a team and sub-committees.
Legrand was nevertheless the animating spirit as it
was he who had chosen his collaborators. The Educational view expressed in the report was bound to be
shared to a large extent by the Minister of Education since Legrand had long shared his political
opinions; indeed Legrand had been removed as the
head of the INRP by the Giscardian Beullac largely
for that very reason.(41) Legrand's proposals
were founded, more solidly than those of Haby, upon
the belief that the education system had not sufficiently tapped the potential to be found in the range
of ability of French schoolchildren. He suggested,
for example, an immediate end to pre-vocational
classes (largely composed of pupils from disadvant-
aged backgrounds) where pupils could go on to vocational training. No pupil should be transferred to
vocational classes unless he specifically requested
it.

The Legrand Report called for the creation in
the first year of completely mixed-ability classes
26 strong at most. However, the front-line subjects
(French, mathematics and the foreign language) would
change the structure of these classes. After the
first month in the case of French and mathematics
and the first term in the case of the foreign language, setting by ability would take place. A year-
group would be taught by a team of teachers specifically assigned to that year and these would decide
when in the week to implement team teaching. A
system of tutors was to be instituted whereby each
of the teachers in a school would become the personal tutor to twelve or fifteen pupils, helping them
in their educational and personal development. This
radical idea of teachers being attached to teams and
working as tutors has far-reaching implications for
teachers' conditions of service. It was proposed
that all teachers in the college should do sixteen
hours teaching plus three hours for tutoring plus
another three hours for team teaching. Such a set-
up would help give a different emphasis to the
assessment of pupils. Instead of relying on termly
and yearly marks, teachers would have a closer
appreciation of the general strengths and weaknesses
of pupils.

The curriculum would also need modification.
The first two years would contain eight subjects:
French, mathematics, a foreign language, human
sciences, natural sciences, arts (music, art and
craft), technical subjects (enseignement polytech-

nique) and PE (including games). Three models were
suggested for the division of time between these but
the report clearly favoured the one which advocated
four 50 minute lessons for each subject. The third
and fourth years would continue with these subjects
and the same time would be devoted to them but an
options system would operate with pupils choosing to
do three hours for each option. On offer would
be Latin, Greek, a second foreign language, or any
other subject in the common core. In the first two
years the preferred model would give a total time of
26 hours and 40 minutes and the second two years
31 hours and 40 minutes.

There seems little revolutionary about the
Legrand proposals but within the context of the
French system and its traditions, this is how they
were often characterised by individuals and the
media. It must be remembered that the proudest
tradition of the secondary system had long been that
of academic excellence based upon streaming. Haby's
mixed-ability bombshell had been quietly defused by
various means within the collège but Legrand had not
only condoned mixed-ability teaching (in most subjects at least) but had lessened divisions within
the collège by calling more strongly for the abolition of the pre-vocational classes and for the development of some common activities with the previously
segregated remedial departments. Team teaching was
even more radical since it had previously been tried
in only a handful of collèges and shook to the very
foundations the idea of the subject specialist which
had always commanded considerable respect. This and
the teacher as a tutor to a restricted group not
only reduced what many regarded as a healthy gap
between pupil and teacher but also struck at the
roots of the teacher hierarchy upon which were based
the nationally agreed conditions of service (dealt
with in a later chapter). Legrand's so-called
balancing of the curriculum increased the time given
to art and craft subjects and to the range of technical subjects that were to be taught under the
title enseignement polytechnique.
However, perhaps the most radical idea of all and
which did not feature among the report's list of
recommendations was that Paris was powerless to
induce change at the wave of a Ministry circular.(42)
Moreover, far from tactfully ignoring the truth,
Savary fully acknowledged it.(43) The result was
that the Ministry asked collèges to volunteer if
they were interested in applying the reforms outlined in the Legrand Report and these schools would

receive special help. Paris had at last officially admitted what had been recognised for a long time: that the education service had grown far too large and complicated for central directives to control it with any precision. The Ministry of Education, under the direction of Savary, chose to encourage de-centralisation - a theme of French government part-icularly strong after the famous events of 1968.

There was a difficulty however at the heart of this latest move to hand over some powers to the participants. Legrand and Savary, by conceding that persuasion was more powerful than directive, were dependent upon an act of faith. It was up to vol-unteers to come forward. They were hoping that teachers in particular knew that their best inter-ests lay in the general themes outlined by the Legrand Report. They were no doubt encouraged (and surprised) by the generally warm welcome for the report from the teachers' unions and the parents' associations. Reservations were expressed of course but the report was usually seen as a step in the right direction. A major factor which must have influenced the teachers was the mitigating of the effects of mixed-ability teaching. Those subjects generally acknowledged to have had the hardest time implementing (or uncomfortably trying to ignore) mixed-ability teaching would be allowed to set pupils by ability and help was to be forthcoming (in what exact form, it was true, was left rather vague) for those prepared to try to modify an unsat-isfactory state of affairs. Savary thus was relying on both negative and positive motivation. Negative in that teachers would be prepared to try to leave behind the failing organisation introduced by the Haby reforms and thus try something new. Positive in that teachers still shared to some extent the Minister's own faith in what the education system could achieve.

The trouble was that Savary was gambling. He was gambling on the good faith of teachers who shared his vision. Many did not. Some reaction was immediately negative and the most usual reason for this was fear; principally fear of loss of status within the teacher hierarchy embodied in their conditions of service which are dealt with in more detail in a later chapter. The proposal that all teachers in the secondary sector should work the same hours meant that those who had worked the least number of hours would have to work more, and since these were the most highly qualified, the accusation that standards were under attack was again made

against the government. Unfortunately for Savary
this attempt to do away with a hierarchical system
that 'has at present no justification'(44) coincided
with another possible major weakness: finance. The
need to pay teachers for equal numbers of hours
worked was probably the most expensive feature of
the reform and thus the most difficult to implement.
Indeed financing the suggestions in the Legrand
Report was to be a major problem at a time when the
socialist government was being forced to cut spending drastically.

Collège organisation

The hierarchy of a collège consists of four members:
the principal, the deputy-head (sous-directeur), the
bursar (usually the intendant) and the conseiller
d'éducation. The principal, who has usually been a
teacher of graduate status, oversees the administration and teaching of the whole school. His tasks are
of course multiple but mainly consist of allocating
classes to teachers (it is therefore he who determines individual teachers' timetables). He is the
go-between for the school and outside bodies and
chairs the school committees. He has only a very
limited power of appointment since all the teaching
posts in a school are allocated by the rectorat. He
must accept whatever teachers are sent. He is also
responsible for the school budget and prepares this
in close cooperation with the bursar. The deputy-
head's role - like that of most deputies in most
organisations - depends rather upon how the principal
sees it, and it can therefore vary from school to
school. In general however he is a PEGC (see the
later chapter on teachers) who assumes the role of
the principal in the latter's absence. He works out
the general timetable, taking into consideration
individual requests from teachers, and organises
cover for absent colleagues. He is responsible for
keeping a check on absenteeism and for the organisation of examinations and marking in general.
    The bursar will have had to have passed the
relevant examinations to get his present position,
the larger the institution usually the better qualified he is. His function is that of accountant and
he is also in charge of the school's ancillary staff
and, through them, of the equipment and general up-
keep of the school. The conseiller d'éducation is
still indissolubly linked solely with the discipline
of pupils in the minds of many Frenchmen although he
has long dropped the more formidable title surveill-

ant général. He still heads the team of surveillants
(often students following courses at the local university) which does all the supervisory tasks such as
playground duty or supervising the (noisy) dinner
queues, and he is still in charge of discipline,
though in this of course he works closely with
teachers. His change of name indicates however that
his role is now conceived as encompassing more than
discipline; thus he is usually in overall charge of
the extra-curricular activities that take place in
school. Again this puts him in contact with teachers
and sometimes allows him to get to know pupils in a
different way from their teachers.
     Four committees help in the running of the
collèges. The School Council (conseil d'établisse-
ment) is presided over by the principal and consists
of five members belonging to the administrative
staff, five elected teacher representatives, five
elected parent representatives, two elected pupil
representatives and five local representatives.
This committee votes the school budget and draws up
the various school rules (règlement interieur). The
latter function does not seem revolutionary but in a
system that has for a very long time been regulated
from Paris, the drawing up of individual school rules
by the school council - an innovation suggested by
Haby in order partly to allow for a certain diversity
within the system - was not without its critics at
first who were fearful that the principle of equality
(equated with uniformity) was under attack. Such
critics need not have worried unduly nor those on
the school council unused to such burdens since there
followed fairly close guidance from the Ministry
about what should feature in such rules. It should
be said at once that these school rules go further
than a reminder to pupils about what to wear and how
to behave. The Ministry at least concedes that they
should cover a wide range of activities relevant to
school life. Besides reaffirming the general nature
of schooling (non-political, tolerant of all beliefs
and so on) the Ministry suggests that the règlement
interieur should include such things as safety
(prevention of fire,accidents; rules for laborator-
ies and workshops; dangerous products); lessons
(attendance, promptness, preparation, the system of
marking to be used); relationships (with pupils and
the family, school records, pupils over eighteen,
role and responsibilities of student representatives);
everyday running of the school (movement between
lessons, school visits, transport, smoking, dress,
permission to leave the premises, damage); staying

for lunch, boarding; discipline (self-discipline, punishments); health (accidents, use of medicines, social diseases); insurance (for various school activities); information and cultural activities (libraries, publications for pupil use, posters, school magazines, activities of clubs); keeping the school rules.(45)

In addition the school council examines the school accounts presented to it by the bursar and is empowered to pass comment on and make suggestions about the teaching. Finally, sitting with reduced membership it is a disciplinary committee in cases when the principal recommends expulsion for a pupil. It has the power to reject the recommendation.

The theory of all those with an interest in the school coming together and working as a team was bound to be modified in the cold light of a committee room. The school council, like most committees, gives rise to factionalism. The school hierarchy is one such faction with the principal rarely being contradicted by his colleagues. The teachers tend to follow the line drawn up by their union. The parents do likewise since they are organised nationally.(46) Parents and teachers, if their solutions to problems vary, do however often agree upon what constitutes the various threats to the education system at different times and they often provide determined pressure groups even to the point of criticising the teaching (in contrast to parent representatives on governing bodies of the state schools in Britain). The representatives of the ancillary staff and office staff do tend to put forward points of view rarely considered previously, and at least they are often heard by the other members whereas the pupil representatives are often just listened to. As for the school rules, despite the Ministry's original conception of these as an opportunity for the school to be positive, collèges do appear to have accentuated the negative instead (pupils must not...). Finally it must be recalled that the committee is really a consultative one and, although it must meet at least once a term, it is the principal who decides when it should meet and it is he who in practice decides the agenda though it is theoretically possible for an extraordinary session to be called if half the council so desires.

A second committee is the Teaching Council (conseil d'enseignement) which brings together all the teachers of one subject. This is chaired not by a head of department since none exists but by the principal. It meets at least once a year and its

business is the relatively straightforward one of
coordinating the teaching of the subject within the
school. Such matters as the choice of books and
teaching methods can be discussed. Once again in
practice the most important influence upon such
meetings is not whether a ministerial decree laid
down such subjects for discussion. What matters is
the attitude of teachers. The tradition of the
qualified professional who knows what is best for
his class clashes somewhat with the idea of working
as a team so the teaching council is often little
inclined to coordinate methods. Freedom of choice
in the matter of textbooks is also limited in that
since the Ministry of Education pays for them, it
insists upon having a say in the costs involved.
This would be far too complicated a business to manage at a local level so the Ministry in fact negoti-
ates with publishers to produce textbooks within a
certain price range. The provision of free textbooks for the collège pupils has been interpreted
by some as a dangerous move towards potential state
control of their content since the three major publishers in the area, Nathan, Bordas and Hachette,
are partly owned through the state holdings in their
parent companies Havas, Paribas and Matra respect-
ively.(47) The argument appears far-fetched.

The third committee is the Teachers' Council
(conseil des professeurs) which consists of all the
members of staff who teach a single class. Evidently therefore each class has its own teachers' council and it meets every term. Once again it is
chaired by the principal. This council discusses
the progress of individual pupils paying particular
attention to the pupil's future choice of courses.
Such meetings have a considerable effect (not always
beneficial) upon the deliberations of the last type
of committee, the Class Council.

The Class Council (conseil de classe) is the
second type of committee which involves pupils and
parents. It has basically the same function as the
Teachers' Council but the wider membership is designed to bring more information to light about individual pupils and to offer a range of viewpoints. Each
class has its corresponding Class Council and it has
as permanent members: the principal and all those
who teach the class, two parent representatives and
two pupil representatives. When they have something
in particular to contribute, various other people
(such as the school doctor or the conseiller
d'éducation) can attend. Unfortunately a potentially
fine opportunity for a greater appreciation on the

part of all members of the point of view of the
others has been missed. The Ministry conceived the
Class Council as the forum for 'the exchange of
information, dialogue, coordination and a stimulus
to further action'(48) but human nature inevitably
modifies ideals. The principal as chairman can
greatly influence the degree of mutual exchange
simply, for example, by encouraging pupils to speak
or ensuring a reasonable amount of time is allowed
to discuss individual cases. In fact, he rarely
appears to do so and in any case the Class Council
often follows a meeting of the Teachers' Council
which always appears to have made the relevant
decisions beforehand. Often parents and pupils are
ushered into the room after the Teachers' Council
has just ended and, as the Ministry has decreed that
the Class Council is there to discuss teaching
matters and 'the results of the work of the Teachers'
Council'(49), the very terms of reference indicate
that a hierarchy is in existence. Teachers in
France - as elsewhere - are often resentful that
non-experts (pupils and parents) are impinging upon
sacred territory. Instead therefore of making an
open and honest attempt to explain their position,
teachers remain over-sensitive to criticism. The
parents and pupils are thus often left with a feeling
of impotence.

Parents for their part can also be disadvant-
aged by the timing of the meeting which can be
shortly after the end of school when most are still
of course in work. They might well lose money by
attending. They also face the difficulty of representing a wide spectrum of opinions held by various
parents and, just as difficult, of finding out what
those opinions are. In fact a general meeting of
parents - a parental equivalent of the Teachers'
Council - would be one of the best ways of canvassing
opinions but these are usually difficult to arrange.
The representatives themselves are not chosen undis-
puted since the places on the Class Councils are
allocated in proportion to the number of votes
received by the nationally organised parents' associations. Individualism is thus not encouraged. The
relative lack of success of the councils can also
sometimes be laid squarely at the door of the parents
themselves since it is not unknown for representatives to become animated at the mention of their own
child's name and moribund at the mention of others.

Perhaps those in the most uncomfortable position are the pupil representatives flanked as they
are by adults supporting sectional interests. Their

lack of experience of committees also puts them at a
disadvantage. Not unnaturally some prefer the quiet
life since taking their role seriously can even lead
to being put firmly in their place.(50)

Besides these various disadvantages the Class
Council faces a difficult task in attempting to discuss properly each individual pupil at one sitting.
The sheer mathematics dictate that discussing a
class, say of 25 pupils, spending only five minutes
on each pupil, would necessitate a two-hour meeting,
and this is without the recommended preliminary
discussion of the class as a whole. Meetings in
excess of two hours are apparently rare(51) so it
can safely be assumed that not every member of the,
say, dozen-strong Class Council contributes fully.
Indeed, given a principal who has already sat
through a meeting with the teachers and who in the
following one is expected to go over the same ground
with non-experts, it would perhaps be surprising to
learn that the Class Council is in fact allowed to
turn into a truly consultative committee. Nevertheless for all its imperfections, it does at least
provide the possibility for the participation of all
parties concerned with the education of pupils.

The CDI

Collèges are increasingly being provided with a CDI
(Centre de documentation et d'information) which is
a mixture of library, resource centre and meeting
place and is looked after (theoretically) by someone
trained for the purpose. The centres were originally conceived at the beginning of the Fifth Republic as an information source for teachers but from
the early seventies their role was widened so that
they now serve anyone concerned with the school,
though in practice this mostly means pupils. Nevertheless they hold an increasingly wide range of materials including those published for pupil guidance
by ONISEP (Office national d'information sur les
enseignements et les professions). They have become
more important as the responsibility for learning
has increasingly devolved over the years upon the
pupils themselves and so they have needed to supply
the growing quest for information not given by
teachers. In fact, the CDI are variable in quality
because they have always suffered from a lack of
funds and they are often partly staffed by untrained
personnel. The facilities tend to be less extensive
in older collèges and all this largely because they
were not viewed for a long time as an essential part

The Collège

of school life. The socialist government elected in
1981 however saw the supply of what are called
documentalistes-bibliothécaires as a priority and
created over 900 new posts in the first three years
of its mandate. The CDI are becoming increasingly
common.

    The four years that are spent at a collège are
divided into two stages each lasting two years: the
observation stage (cycle d'observation) and the
orientation stage (cycle d'orientation).(52) For a
supposedly logical nation the French persist in the
illogically reverse numbering of their classes: the
entrants to the collège thus go into the classe de
sixième and continue after that into the classe de
cinquième, the classe de quatrième, and finally into
the classe de troisième. Unfortunately for the
reverse numerical system the courses at the lycée
last three years and so the last class is not logic-
ally named the first (la première) but the terminale.
    All pupils follow the same syllabus in the
sixième and the cinquième in the collège. The subjects and the number of hours spent on each per week
are: French (five hours); mathematics (three hours);
modern language (three hours); history, geography,
economics, civics (three hours); experimental
sciences (three hours); artistic education (two
hours); manual and technical education (two hours);
PE and games (three hours). Thus the normal timetable for a pupil in the first two years of secondary school lasts 24 hours with the possibility of
this being 28 if he is involved to the maximum in
the core subjects with soutien or approfondissement.
Lessons usually last 55 minutes with five minutes
between.
    The subjects are divided into three groups.
Firstly, those that are called the three fundamental
subjects: French, mathematics and a foreign language.
It is because these three are regarded as basic to a
pupil's development and because it is maintained
that their development is linear in that each new
step depends upon what has been learnt before that
they benefit from the possibility of an extra hour
each. The second group of subjects (disciplines
d'éveil) which includes all the remainder apart from
PE are supposed to exercise a pupil's intelligence
and powers of observation and reflection. The third
group, particularly concerned with the physical
development of children, is composed of PE and games.
    In the third and fourth years pupils continue

with the same curriculum but spend an extra three hours (two hours if they opt to spend extra time on their first language) on one of the following: Latin, Greek, a second foreign language or one of three technological options (broadly, industrial or economic). They may, if they wish, also study another one from the list of options. Depending upon the option chosen, upon how much soutien or approfondissement is organised and upon whether an optional extra subject is taken, a pupil's total number of weekly hours in the cycle d'orientation can theoretically vary between 24½ and 32½ hours, though the usual figure would normally be somewhere in the middle of the two extremes. The small percentage of time devoted to optional subjects is a deliberate educational and political decision. Pupils who follow the courses at the collèges between the ages of eleven and fifteen are in effect doing a common core of subjects for by far the greater part of their career. Apart from the hope that all pupils will be in possession of a culture common to the majority of future French citizens, the aim of the common curriculum is to enable those who intend continuing their studies at the lycée for the baccalauréat to have equality of choice between the various courses offered there and not to have prematurely debarred themselves from a career which later appeals by ill-considered early specialisation.

Remedial Education
Remedial sections or SES (Sections d'éducation spécialisée) were created experimentally in 1965, then on a wide scale after 1967.(53) They are attached to certain collèges and cater for pupils from twelve to sixteen years of age. In principle such pupils have an IQ between 65 and 80 though this is not the sole criterion. Increasingly over the years more notice has been taken of a child's individual progress. The affectation of a child to a SES depends upon the decisions taken by a committee of people particularly concerned with special education in the secondary sector called the CCSD (Commission de circonscription du second degré) which is composed of inspectors, teachers, doctors and parents. There are usually more candidates for the SES than places available.
In principle each SES has 90 pupils and the education dispensed differs somewhat depending upon whether pupils are under or over fourteen years of age. Both sections have official timetables which

indicate the number of hours to be spent on what.
Thus the section composed of the younger pupils has
its week divided thus: acquisition of techniques of
communication (reading, oral expression), arithmetic
basic logical exercises, measuring (ten hours);
practical study of natural and human environment,
civics, highway code, practical introduction to society (six hours); introduction to the arts (four
hours); craft (four hours); PE (two hours). The
total of 26 hours is supplemented by reasonably long
recreational periods. Evidently, a large degree of
initiative is left in the hands of the teachers and
a certain amount of overlap occurs between those
areas in the above timetable.

After the age of fourteen in addition to continuing with their general education, the pupils are
introduced gradually to the world of work and engage
in pre-vocational and vocational activities, including visits to various places of work such as factories and offices. Different SES can have different
specialisms depending upon the type of area in which
they are situated and depending upon the sorts of
jobs available there, but most SES attempt to train
their pupils for low-grade work, for example in
mechanics or as machine workers.

The SES accommodation is sometimes self-contained though this can bring complaints about being
cut off from the rest of the collège. Theoretically
the SES pupils can be reintegrated into an LEP but
this is not common. They may also study for a CEP
(Certificat d'éducation professionnelle) - the qualification linked to some specific economic need of
the area and designed for pupils in difficulties -
or a vocational qualification, but again a pupil in
an SES rarely obtains the latter.

Indeed the lack of qualifications among SES
pupils highlights one of the major weaknesses of
this type of education: the insufficient preparation
for a job. The fact that pupils spend a smaller
proportion of their time in training than those
pupils who go on to a vocational course in a lycée
d'enseignement professionnel (which will be dealt
with in the following chapter) obviously puts them
at a marked disadvantage. Another complaint often
voiced about the SES is that they lack enough
qualified staff, particularly, for example, specialists in technical drawing or in a variety of crafts
or sport. The latest proposals embodied in the
Legrand report advocates a much closer cooperation
between the SES and the rest fo the collège, eventually leading to a complete integration with the

main stream but with ability setting where necessary.

Orientation

The emphasis in the word _démocratisation_ has gradually shifted from the idea of equal physical access
to that of real equality of treatment. And this is
where _orientation_ comes in. Its function has always
been to match aspirations to courses and careers.
The various choices opened up to pupils as they
progress through the system should allow those capable and desirous of staying on in the mainstream
of school to do so. Now although it is accepted
that not all pupils are equally endowed intellectually, the criticism of the French system has been
(and still is) that pupils are guided out of the
mainstream _collège_ studies into pre-vocational and
vocational classes (and thereby into the world of
work or unemployment) too early. In practice
orientation is conditioned exclusively by the marks
a pupil obtains in his studies whereas theoretically
it should in some measure at least be independent
of them. To make matters worse, those who are ushered into those courses which lead earliest to the outside world are overwhelmingly from the lower end of
the social scale. To many Frenchmen this has long
been unacceptable and much effort has gone into trying to moderate the almost deterministic cycle of
under-privilege. This has by no means been the
exclusive concern of the Left. Haby's noble attempt
to treat all pupils equally by legislating for
mixed-ability classes is such an example. However
orientation, runs the complaint, is nothing but a
device for filtering out the under-privileged as
soon as possible since those in difficulty are never
offered the same options as the others. Such state-
ments by the Ministry of Education as, for example,
in a decree which followed the Haby law declaring
that 'the possibilities for _orientation_ are the same
for all pupils'(54) are at the very least pious.
How then is the system of _orientation_ put into practice?

Orientation theoretically begins at the end of
the second year of the _collège_ when pupils opt for
courses that either take them into the third year at
the _collège_ or to an LEP to study for a vocational
qualification or into a pre-vocational class, the
CPPN (Classe _pré-professionnelle de niveau_) or the
CPA (Classe _préparatoire à l'apprentissage_). Apart
from the first option, pupils must be at least fourteen in the year that they go into any of these

classes (fifteen in the case of CPA) which means
that if they are to enter after the second year at
the _collège_ they must be behind in their year group.
In fact because of the system of repeating a year,
pupils can be of the right age at the end of the
first year at the _collège_ (or even by the end of the
primary school). Those who object to the present
system of _orientation_ claim that what is happening
is not _orientation_ at all but selection (a word
often abhorred in the French educational system).
No real choice is involved. Pupils opt not to
continue in the _collège_ mainstream because they feel
alienated. They act out of a sense of failure
rather than out of any positive motivation.

Figures vary from year to year (and from area
to area) but, roughly speaking, only 60 per cent of
the initial intake to the _collège_ system goes from
the second into the third year. The second year is
therefore a decisive one. There is rich material
here for a Marxist analysis: the capitalist system
needs failures to fill the menial posts and the
education system supplies them from the lowest
classes. The elite meanwhile perpetuates its hold
on power. But if premature _orientation_ into apprenticeships or vocational courses in an LEP has been
criticised, it is the CPPN above all which has come
in for the greatest hostility.

From the very beginning of the Fifth Republic
when the secondary system was being reformed, a
major problem has been what to do with the weakest
pupils. When streaming was still the order of the
day, those in the bottom groups, the _classes de
transition_, who had not succeeded in going up into
the next section, were put into _classes pratiques_.
The curriculum and methods were adapted to the pupils
and included lessons in the basic subjects so that a
reasonable level might be reached and in wide-ranging
pre-vocational studies such as woodwork, metalwork
and basic electrical engineering. They were unsucc-
essful for several reasons. They were poorly
equipped and the staff assigned to them were often
unqualified to teach such classes. In addition they
led nowhere in particular and certainly were not
vocational in nature.

Since the early seventies the so-called practical courses have been progressively replaced by the
CPPN and CPA with both these being angled much more
towards the choice of a career and seen as two
stages in the same progression. The aim of both
classes is similar in that they continue a pupil's
general education (though there is greater emphasis

than before upon adapting the subject-matter to
individuals) and they progressively prepare a pupil
for a job. The CPPN allows a pupil to come into
contact with the theory and practice of a range of
jobs and, after he has made a final choice, the CPA
allows him to spend a total of half the year out
working. The days of the pre-vocational class seemed over when the Haby reforms stipulated that all
pupils in the college were to receive the same education. However the 1975 law also laid down that the
last two years of the first cycle of secondary study
could contain pre-vocational classes and a later
circular improved their organisation.(55) The fact
is however that such measures only tinker with a
problem that remains as obstinate as ever. The CPPN
is widely regarded as little less than a slough of
despond. It is where failures end up. Its pupils
have struggled and lost and in addition are quite
possibly those who could not be accommodated (because
of a lack of places there) in a class for remedial
pupils or in one especially set up to help immigrant
children. They might have tried for a place on a
vocational course but have been turned down because
of their poor academic record. The hope is therefore
that the CPPN will prepare pupils adequately so that
they may eventually get on to a vocational course.
In fact only about 50 per cent do (1980-1) whilst
30 percent quit school unqualified and 20 per cent
repeat the year. The latter statistic in particular
makes some of the information to pupils given out by
the government agency ONISEP seem optimistic when its
1981-2 brochure on pupil orientation claims that a
second year in the CPPN is only done 'exception-
ally'.(56)

The Legrand Report renews the attack upon the
pre-vocational classes calling not only for an end
to them immediately when there is an LEP for pupils
to go to but also for a phasing out over three years
of the LEP option at all at the end of the second
year. What appears to rankle with the critics of the
CPPN apart from the resigned - or indeed hostile -
attitude of the pupils of such classes, is the disproportionate percentage of children there who come
from the lower socio-economic groups. But it is
easier to analyse what is wrong than to implement
solutions. The immediate abolishing of pre-vocational classes would do no more for those in difficulties
than the immediate introduction of any other measure
such as mixed-ability teaching for all. Educational
handicap cannot be made to disappear overnight. The
CPPN is only the physical manifestation of a multi-

faceted failure and one which of course is certainly
not confined to France. If the CPPN were proscribed
immediately, it is unlikely that the collège could
even accommodate its pupils. Even with a greater
political will to change the system, there seems
little any government could do to effect real change
since the division of youngsters into successes and
failures depending upon the type of course they
undertake (and eventually what sort of job they
obtain) happens because people's attitudes are
conditioned towards regarding certain types of work
as more prestigious than others.

Before leaving the subject of orientation in
the collèges, it should be said that the other
important stage for its implementation comes at the
end of the fourth year, the last year of the collège.
This is where the first orientation should be taking
place if, that is, the cycle d'orientation did what
it was supposed to. The possibilities open to a
pupil are basically the same as at the end of the
second year. He can continue his studies in the
mainstream and go to a lycée and there choose a
baccalauréat option or do a short vocational course
(though the range of possibilities widens considerably at this stage) or leave school. These options
will be dealt with in more detail in the next
chapter.

NOTES

    1.   For a discussion of the BEPC see Valerie
Dundas- Grant, 'Attainment at 16+: the French
Perspective' Comparative Education, March 1975.
    2.   D.Zimmermann(ed.), Questions-Réponses sur
les collèges, p.13.
    3.   Ibid.
    4.   'Exposé des motifs de l'ordonnance
relative à la scolarité obligatoire et du décret
portant réforme de l'enseignement public', Education
nationale, 8 jan. 1959.
    5.   That is, it would apply for the first time
to pupils who would be six after 1 January 1959.
    6.   'Les points majeurs de la Réforme de
l'Enseignement', Education nationale, 8 jan. 1959.
    7.   André Le Gall declared that the reforms
'impliquent qu'au long des deux années du cycle
d'observation, et même aussi longtemps qu'il sera
possible, nul ne se heurt au cloisonnement des
enseignements et des programmes'. Education nationale, 8 jan. 1959, p.2.

8.   See his speech to the National Assembly on Wednesday, 20 May, 1965.
9.   Ministère de l'Education Nationale, Répères, p.49.
10.   Circulaire du 3 mai, 1963.
11.   Circulaires: 3.5.63; 28.9.63; 5.1.65.
12.   For other criticisms of the carte scolaire see Nicholas Beattie, 'The French Schools' Map in Context', Comparative Education, vol.17, No.3, 1981.
13.   This local pride plus a centralised decision-making process helps explain why the number of CES rose rapidly. Some commentators have compared (unfavourably) Britain's slower move towards the creation of comprehensive schools. See, for example, Guy Neave, 'The Reform of Secondary Education in France', Forum, Spring 1975.
14.   Circulaire du 11 oct. 1971.
15.   La Démocratie française, p.56.
16.   La Réforme du système éducatif, p.27.
17.   La Démocratie française, p.66.
18.   'Dans les collèges, les élèves sont repartis, sans distinction, en classes constituées pour l'année scolaire.' Art.6. Décret du 1 déc. 1976.
19.   Change in this sector had become so frequent that many found it difficult to keep up. An article in the weekly L'Express purporting to outline the latest developments for 'parents et enfants qui ne savent plus où ils sont' gave the following list of subjects which would constitute the timetable for schoolchildren in the first years of the collège: 'Français, mathématiques, une langue vivante, histoire et géographie, sciences physiques et naturelles, éducation artistique, éducation nouvelle (sic) et technique. Soit vingt et une heures de cours par semaine.' ('Où va l'éducation?' 11-17 sept. 1978, p.50). Besides not mentioning that civics was to be included in history and geography lessons and misprinting 'éducation manuelle', the list omitted PE and games which in fact brought the total of weekly hours to 24 (and this without the possible addition of three hours' soutien).
20.   See Roger Ikor, 'Les fiches au feu!' Le Monde, 26.8.77.
21.   The Ministry of Education brought out a special edition of its information bulletin aimed specifically at the pupils. See Le Courrier de l'Education (Spécial élèves), No.28, déc. 1977.
22.   Arrêté du 5 juillet, 1978.
23.   Le Monde, 31.5.77.
24.   All supply teachers would be re-employed; 450 new classes in nursery and primary schools would

be opened (in addition to those provided for in the budget); 25,000 first forms would have 24 pupils or less (there had been 16,700 the year before); no secondary classes would have more than 30 pupils (there had been 7,900 in 1976-7) and classes with 24 and over would number 6,000. 'Une rentrée scolaire sans problèmes?' Le Monde, 9.9.77.

25. Décret du 28 déc. 1976. Art.6.

26. General advice had come from the Ministry (Circulaire du 28 mars, 1977) but what teachers could do in their own subject depended upon patchy in-service activities organised in their area and individual initiative.

27. See Jean Dresch, 'Les surprises des manuels d'histoire et de géographie en sixième', Le Monde, 3.1.78.

28. 'Sans préjuger tel ou tel ouvrage, on peut affirmer que les nouveaux manuels dégagent mieux les points essentiels de chaque leçon, et cela dans une présentation beaucoup plus accessible à de jeunes élèves.' La Réforme du système éducatif français, p.111.

29. 'un ministre,' declared the SNI, 'qui a, depuis longtemps, perdu toute crédibilité.' Le Nouvel Observateur, 28.2.77, p.23.

30. 15 June, 1978. Indeed in the June before his reform was due to be introduced, Haby himself had said to the Commission des affaires culturelles, familiales et sociales of the National Assembly that headmasters had considerable latitude in setting up a mixed-ability first form, Le Monde, 2.7.77.

31. 'C'est à demander si le système éducatif (...) n'est pas devenu une gigantesque machine à fabriquer des cancres,' L'Express, 27.9.80.

32. 'L'Ecole: ce qui ne va pas', Le Nouvel Observateur, 11.9.82.

33. See the interview with Antoine Prost, Le Nouvel Observateur, 11.9.82.

34. Cahiers de l'Education nationale, jan. 1982.

35. Dominique Paty, Douze collèges en France, enquête sur le fonctionnement des collèges publics aujourd'hui.

36. Cahiers de l'Education nationale, juin 1983.

37. Such projects go under the name of PAE or Projets d'actions éducatives and were extended to primary schools in January 1983.

38. A Ministry of Education study (1980) of mixed-ability teaching in the first form showed that only about 60 per cent of classes were organised as

Haby had intended. Le Monde 4.2.83.

39. See Jean Binon in Pour un collège démocratique, p.261.

40. For example, that of 7 déc. 1978 made it clear that not all pupils leaving the second year would go on to mixed-ability third years.

41. Note Legrand's support of the Left in an interview for Le Monde, 20.1.83.

42. 'Les modifications proposées ne sauraient être imposées du sommet par voie réglementaire.' Pour un collège démocratique, p.170.

43. He included the following among other lessons to be learnt: 'Ne pas imposer brutalement une réforme arrêtée dans le détail au niveau central. Ne pas croire que les problèmes se résolvent avec les textes quand ils se résolvent avec les hommes.' Press conference, 1 Feb. 1983.

44. Pour un collège démocratique, p.122.

45. Circulaire du 18.7.77.

46. The two most powerful are the Fédération des Parents d'Elèves de l'Enseignement Public and the Fédération des Conseils des Parents d'Elèves des Ecoles Publiques.

47. 'Livres scolaires: la gratuité au rabais', L'Express, 16.10.81.

48. Circulaire du 14 nov. 1977.

49. Art.24. Décret 76-1305.

50. See 'Que cachent les conseils de classe?' L'Express, 11.4.81. This is a highly critical article though supportive of the pupil's position.

51. Daniel Zimmermann(ed.) Questions-réponses sur les collèges, p.58.

52. Orientation is impossible to translate into a single English word but, briefly, it means the guidance of pupils into the most appropriate courses. For the secondary pupil, however, it has the negative inference of guiding the less able into vocational subjects.

53. Circulaire du 27 déc. 1967.

54. Décret du 26 déc. 1976. Art.17.

55. Circulaire du 8 juin, 1977.

56. Après la classe de cinquième, p.8.

Chapter 3

THE <u>LYCEE</u>

Although the term <u>lycée</u> covers several categories of
school which educate pupils beyond the <u>collège</u> and
although there are evidently variations within each
category caused by such factors as the area in which
a school is situated, its accommodation and the
nature of the individuals who work within it, what
strikes an outsider is the degree of uniformity of
the <u>lycées</u>: the same buildings, severely utilitarian,
with many of the older ones not dissimilar to army
barracks; the same teaching methods reminiscent of
the university lecture theatre. These characteristics are largely attributable to the long tradition
of centralised control, to the attitude that the
state knows (and therefore disposes) best. But to
many French people such uniformity is of minor
importance ranking as an acceptable inconvenience so
long as the <u>lycées</u> remain academic power-houses.
The <u>lycées</u> (and here the LEP must be excluded) are
expected to make their pupils work so that the nation may be provided with its future middle and top
management as well as its future leaders. Unlike
the state sector in Britain, that in France does not
have to resist any challenge from a private sector
for the country's brightest minds. People from all
walks of life expect no better education than that
which is provided by the state <u>lycée</u>.
    The academic tradition has been less easy to
maintain as the years have gone by. This is
largely because of the increase in numbers of those
following academic courses from age fifteen on. In
1960-1 there were some 420,000 pupils undertaking
such courses. This number rose to some 850,000 in
1970-1 and to well over a million in 1980-1. Only
gradually (some critics contend that it is impercept-
ibly) have these types of <u>lycée</u> adapted to the new
clientele and we shall later examine the most recent

efforts to tailor courses to the influx. When the
discontent of university students overflowed into
the lycées in 1968 there followed a period when
pupils were allowed greater freedoms and more say in
the running of their schools. These freedoms remain
part and parcel of the lycée today but 1968 was a
long time ago and pupils now seem less prone to
challenge authority. The lycées seem to have ridden
the storm of that contentious generation. They have
adapted their surface conditions but fundamentally
pupils' attitudes remain unchanged; they still treat
the lycée as a supermarket where they go for what
they want and leave as soon as possible. Not that
reforms have not been tried. It was in the early
seventies when Joseph Fontanet was Minister of Education that the idea of schools devoting ten per cent
of their time to non-academic subjects was introduced. This was in order to counter the exclusive
concentration upon examinations and the tunnel vision
provoked by the baccalauréat. Various approaches
were tried by many lycées such as the creation of
clubs or the organising of visits to various places
of interest but eventually such efforts were largely
abandoned as the vision of those in the lycées
narrowed again. It would be too harsh to say that
all lycées were permeated with a feeling of resignation but this feeling is not rare particularly
among the pupils. The lycée is where one works.
For most pupils real life is elsewhere.

The term lycée is well known outside France but
little save the name itself is familiar to many
The fact is that it covers a wide range of institutions: the lycée d'enseignement général,(1) the lycée
technique(2) and the lycée d'enseignement professionnel (LEP). Each of these differs form the others
depending upon which of the four types of course(3)
is taught in them. The course for the baccalauréat
de l'enseignement secondaire lasts three years and
is divided into two basic sorts (which are further
sub-divided): the more general one (taught in the
lycée général) which is considered solely as the
first stage of higher education studies, and the
vocational baccalauréat (BTn), taught in the technical lycée, which in addition to being a passport
to further study, can theoretically be used immediately on the job market. In recent years because
of the increased difficulty in finding employment
this latter use has declined somewhat. Many lycées
(called lycées polyvalents) now teach both the
general and technical baccalauréats. The brevet de
technicien(BT) lasts three years and is also

vocationally orientated. The _certificat d'aptitude
professionnelle_(CAP) and the _brevet d'enseignement
professionnel_(BEP) both train students for more or
less specific jobs and both are taught exclusively
in the LEP.
One other type of _lycée_ should be mentioned.
The Ministry of Agriculture maintains a network of
lycées d'enseignement professionnel agricole(LEPA)
whose courses lead to the agricultural _baccalauréat_
and qualifications for less prestigious jobs in
agriculture. Thus, like the _lycée technique_, the
LEPA sends pupils either into higher education or
directly (and literally) into the field. Some other
ministries also have small networks of schools which
train people specifically for jobs within their
ambit. The Ministry of Health trains hospital administrators and nurses (among others), the Ministry of
Defence through the armed forces trains personnel
for a wide range of jobs and the Ministry of Employment has a particular responsibility for the retraining of young adults. The state runs some 400
general _lycées_, 300 technical _lycees_, 500 _lycées
polyvalents_ and 1,300 LEPs.

School Administration
Those members of the school hierarchy who are responsible for the administrative running of the _lycée_
correspond closely to those already mentioned in the
collège chapter. The Headmaster of the LEP is known
as the _directeur_ though this changes in the case of
the other types of _lycée_ to _proviseur_. It is interesting to note that the female incumbent of this
post in all types of _lycée_ is usually called a
directrice because there is no female form in French
for _proviseur_. However, this might soon change.
The Socialist government under François Mitterrand
with its Minister for Women's Rights, Evette Roudy,
who in April 1984 sought to bring relief to those
women having to labour under a masculine-gender job,
set up a commission to supply female forms for those
posts that have only a masculine name.
Naturally such a key post has considerable
potential for good or evil and the atmosphere in a
lycée can depend to a large extent upon the personality of its Head. Nevertheless the post is often
viewed as a purely administrative one and the fact
that the curriculum is largely externally determined
and monitored and that the Head has no power of
appointment or dismissal of staff reinforces this
trait. In recent years under the Ministers of

Education Fontanet and Haby this image of a man
apart from the chalk-face concerns of the teachers
has, if anything, been strengthened by various
Ministry circulars. But the Head's position is far
from all-powerful. Haby had wanted to incorporate
into the Head's responsibilities an official right
to reprimand staff but opposition was sufficiently
strong, particularly from teachers' unions, for the
idea to be dropped. Despite occasional instances of
Heads digging their heels in and quarrelling with
sections of school staffs, the more usual picture is
of a man who is at the centre of various influences
and who tries keeping the peace by adopting compromise rather than conflict as his method of procedure.
In a way he is caught in a difficult position in
that he is ultimately responsible for what goes on
in his school, yet he must for ever balance different interests. The casualty in all this tends to be
the lead he could offer in curricular areas. Constantly preoccupied with running an efficient administration and applying the flow of instructions from
a range of central and regional government bodies,
the quality of teaching in the lycée is something
virtually beyond his control. In any case, curriculum matters fall mainly into the purview of the
Inspectorate as we shall see in the last chapter.
The Head has the right to go into a teacher's classroom but tends to reserve such visits for the times
when the Inspector calls, and even then many a Head
would feel chary about taking up this opportunity.
Moreover the latest report on the lycées published
at the end of 1983, whilst recognising the capital
importance of the proviseur and suggesting many
changes for this type of school, remains tentative
and vague about this aspect of the Head's role.(4)
The status quo in other words is accepted.
    Little need be added about the other key figures
in the administrative hierarchy of the lycée since
they differ hardly at all from those already treated
in the previous chapter. The Head's deputy is
called the censeur (except in the LEP) thereby
retaining the name first given in 1803 when he had
the job of vetting all books, drawings and engravings
which came into the school. The retention of the
nineteenth-century name has misled some modern
commentators like John Ardagh who has taken it to
mean a 'disciplinary official'(5). The intendant
has particular responsibility for the financial
running of the lycée and the conseiller d'éducation,
who adopts the role of the censeur in the LEP, for
the general well-being of pupils. The one post

that is not found in the <u>collège</u> or <u>lycée général</u>
is the <u>chef de travaux</u>(6). He is the central figure
in vocational education since he knows the ins and
outs of the practical subjects - which the administ-
rator-<u>proviseur</u> rarely does. He liaises with outside commercial or industrial concerns and takes
part in the examining of pupils who sit for vocational qualifications. He attempts to ensure a match
between the theoretical and practical sides of
various courses and to do the same for the vocational courses and those designed to continue the pupils'
general education.

Changes in the lycées

The arrival of the Fifth Republic heralded fundamental changes for the whole system of <u>lycées</u> and it is
worthwhile outlining briefly the major ones, first
for the <u>lycée général</u>, second for the <u>lycée tech-
nique</u> and thirdly for the LEP. In the late 1950s
the <u>lycée général</u> catered mainly for those aged
between eleven and eighteen. Some <u>lycées</u> had
younger classes attached to them which prepared
their pupils for the examinations for entry into the
<u>lycée</u> proper. It was a time, it will be remembered,
when many pupils might well continue their education
in the primary school and not move into a true secondary school at all. The beginning of the end of
this system came in 1969 when the Berthoin reform
raised the school-leaving age to sixteen and observation cycles were set up for pupils aged eleven and
over. As we have seen, the CEG began to change the
face of secondary eductaion but it was in 1963 with
the creation of the CES that the role of the <u>lycée</u>
was irrevocably altered. Slowly but surely the
<u>lycées</u> began to take pupils only after they had
completed the first cycle of their secondary education in the <u>collège</u>. Pupils thus were at least
fifteen before they started the second cycle of
their secondary schooling.

The major changes to the <u>collège</u> undertaken by
the Minister of Education Christian Fouchet in the
early and mid-sixties heralded (less dramatic)
changes in the <u>lycées</u> of the period. This was the
time when the literary <u>baccalauréat</u> was still the
most prestigious and Latin or Greek was necessary
before being admitted to it. One consequence of this
was that those pupils who had not received their
education in a traditional <u>lycée</u> were unable to opt
for that section since no ancient languages were
taught in the CEG. Such pupils were obliged to

follow the scientific section. Indeed the baccalauréat up to the end of the sixties was dominated by
these two sections: the literary and the scientific.
The latter however was not very appealing to most
pupils whether from the CEG or not since it revelled
in abstraction. It had adapted to rapid scientific
advance by increasing the amount to be covered in
the syllabuses and cutting down on the non-scientific
parts of the course. Almost inevitably pupils were
obliged to grasp less and less about more and more
and their learning was often criticised for being
superficial.(7)

In other words the lycée and the baccalauréat
were still very much geared to the production of an
elite in an ivory tower. The massive increase in
the school population as it rolled towards that
tower made the latter look singularly shakey. Syllabuses were altered and new options introduced.
Economics, social science and an extensive range of
technical options were brought in(8) and achieved
the status of fully fledged courses as one part of
the attempt to open up the lycée to a changing world.

Elitism was weakened to some extent by more
being done to prevent pupils' early specialisation.
Thus for example after the 1965 reforms an ancient
language was no longer required to study for the
literary option of the baccalauréat. The ability to
quote classical works had for many years been
regarded, as Dr Johnson had put it, as being the
parole of literary men all over the world. Indeed
suggestions to lessen the status of Latin and Greek
by making them optional rather than compulsory had
always been fiercely opposed. By the mid-sixties
however even the teachers of these subjects found
the prospect of teaching willing rather than unwilling pupils more alluring and when the change came
little opposition was voiced.

Another important innovation during the Fouchet
era was the broadening of the first year baccalauréat
courses. Before 1965 pupils had a choice of eight
courses, each leading to specific baccalauréats.
From the mid-sixties pupils chose one of three and
it was only in the second year that the more specialised courses began.

Laudable as these reforms were, it was not long
before they in turn became the object of criticism.
The broad division of the courses became too complex
in their detail and they were still attacked for
being too discrete with little or no cross-fertilis-
ation between subjects. This was exacerbated by the
two literary and scientific sections being confined

to the classical lycée and the third - the vocational section - to the technical lycée. No doubt the
events of May 1968 (in which lycée pupils played
their full part) added to the government's anxiety
to remedy any cause that might again give rise to
such social foment. The late sixties and early
seventies tended to be a jittery time for governments
and as early as 1971 the Minister of Education
Olivier Guichard was putting forward proposals to
continue the work begun by the 1965 reforms. He
suggested a timetable of subjects which would be
studied by all pupils in their first year of baccalauréat studies. These should consist of what he
termed (more for the sake of symmetry than clarity)
the four basic languages: French, mathematics, a
foreign language and PE (the last presumably being
body language). The familiar complaint was that
pupils studying science could not express themselves
satisfactorily and that pupils studying literature
lacked rigour and logic. Such complaints by the
French about their own system may come as a surprise
to those who have been used to admiring the baccalauréat precisely because it offered a range of
experience but the mere fact that all pupils did
some French and some science was not regarded as
being proof against philistinism if the balance and
the detail of the mixture were not correct.
    The second feature of the reforms called for by
Guichard was the creation of a series of optional
subjects from which pupils could choose in order to
enhance personal choice. The third feature was the
creation of a new 'subject' which gave pupils the
opportunity to discuss the modern world.(9)
    In addition it had long been felt that pupils
had been obliged to study courses on entry which
effectively meant that they committed themselves to
options before they had time to reflect upon what
was best for them. One commentator stated baldly
in 1975: 'Upon entry to the lycée the options are
numerous, the syllabuses specialised, future movement from one course to another difficult. In the
majority of cases the choice which is made is practically irreversible.'(10) Major reform was to come
in 1980 but before dealing with this we shall first
look at the development of technical education.

Technical Education
As in other countries, technical education does not
enjoy equal status with non-vocational education,
although it has become somewhat more highly regarded

under the Fifth Republic. Constant reminders by
politicians and education officials about the equal
value, nay nobility, of technical subjects have had
as much to do with this however as righteous exhort-
ation usually has. The principal impulse for such
support has been the increasing realisation that a
developing advanced economy depends upon a work force
with ever more refined skills. This has worked to
the advantage of technical education in that it is
believed that in order to raise the skill threshold
pupils' general education must also be of a higher
standard. Thus whereas at the beginning of the
Fifth Republic pupils were allowed to begin vocational courses immediately upon leaving primary school,
they were soon required to obtain some secondary
education at least. The Berthoin reforms not only
began to open education to all, they also began the
process of integration and rationalisation of technical education as a whole. In 1960 the various
types of schools dispensing vocational education
were brought under one roof and henceforth called
the lycées techniques.(11) In addition the centres
d'apprentissage became collèges d'enseignement
technique which in turn became known from the autumn
of 1977 (thanks to the Haby reforms) as lycées
d'enseignement professionnel. Brand new courses
such as the BEP were created to develop a high level
of skill and several technical subjects were granted
the status of baccalauréat by the reform of 1965.
Courses in technical lycées were also brought closer
to those in general lycées.
        This deliberate policy of upgrading technical
education has on the whole been successful. There
has been a general decrease in the number of pupils
leaving school without any vocational qualification
and numbers following technical courses have grown
greatly.(12) Certainly the education system can
refute charges occasionally brought against it by
the French media that little is being done by the
schools to prepare pupils for finding jobs. The
fact is that pupils have been increasingly better
qualified over the years.
        In a way however the technical education sector
needs to be on its toes to refute such charges if
confidence in it is not to wane for, unlike many
advanced industrialised countries, France has long
decided to place the onus of vocational training
upon schools rather than upon industry. Nonetheless
it would be overstating the case to say that the
extensive vocational training network in France is
the result of a consistent political will since its

expansion over the years was very much a response to
the lack of enthusiasm by French industry to enter
the area of vocational training. Whatever the reasons for its present shape, the technical sector of
the education system displays advantages and disadvantages of being closely involved with the Ministry
of Education. A reasonably coherent number of technical courses has been built up and fairly evenly
distributed throughout the country. The network of
options could of course be more extensive in many
areas so that pupils followed courses they really
wished to instead of being obliged to take their
second or third choice, as many have to now. The
fact that the state has a large stake in the technical field has also meant that pupils' education
has not been prematurely fixed exclusively upon
competence in a particular vocational skill but that
pupils have benefited from a range of more general
subjects. The involvement of the Ministry of Education has also meant that such matters as health and
safety regulations have been enforced.
  On the other hand trying to cater for the
enormous number of job options in the outside world
within the school system almost inevitably means
that schools trail behind the demands of industry.
To keep schools sufficiently well equipped in up-to-
date machinery needed to give pupils a proper idea
of modern requirements is simply beyond the Ministry
of Education. This is hardly surprising since
industry and commerce themselves can find it difficult to raise the capital needed for investment.
  Renewal is called for not only in machinery but
in many other aspects. The very existence of a
business may depend upon its adaptability. No such
pressure is exercised upon schools. The gap between
what happens in the outside world and in the practical classes in schools can become dangerously wide.
Yet it is no simple matter to adapt teachers and
equipment. It is a difficult balancing act for the
education system to master. On the one hand schools
must keep in contact with the needs of industry yet
on the other they must not become subservient to it
since pupils are at school to be educated rather
than just trained. The 1980 reforms of the lycées
led to a strengthening of Education in this wider
sense.

Baccalauréat courses
Since 1981-2 most pupils in the lycées (apart from
the LEP) have a common first year of studies. Virt-

ually all follow the same syllabuses in each of:
French, history, geography (including civics), a
foreign language, mathematics, physical science,
natural science, physical education and games. To
some extent therefore the concern often expressed,
for example by Giscard in the previous chapter, that
French school children should share the same culture
is being satisfied by this common core. But pressure for specialisation is just as powerful an influence at this stage in a French pupil's schooling and
this is catered for by a range of optional subjects
and a further set of complementary options which may
be chosen theoretically out of pure interest. Now a
glance at Table 3.1 shows how greatly the timetable
can differ between pupils according to which options
they choose. Clearly those who take the first group
of obligatory options will have a heavier timetable
than those who choose the second and thus it might
be assumed that, not being simple-minded, pupils
would opt to leave the technical subjects strictly
alone. They might indeed if they were given the
choice but they are not. The type of final qualification desired determines to a large extent the
choice of options. All the BTn and BT have as their
foundation course the technical options. This in
itself is not surprising since the degree of depth
of understanding of a subject area will depend
largely upon the time spent studying it. Nevertheless this has the consequence of dividing those
studies partly orientated towards the world of work
from those with a less specific bias. What this does
of course is to reaffirm the general impression that
so-called technical subjects are less noble. However there is a real difficulty here for anyone who
wishes to adopt what appears to be the simple exped-
ient of postponing the technical options and thereby
perhaps instituting a first year in which all pupils
study identical subjects. The BTn and BT have a
certain currency on the job market because employers
know what they are getting: three years' advanced
study with increasing specialisation in a job-relat-
ed activity. If specialisation were postponed, the
BTn and BT would be devalued in the eyes of the
employers and these qualifications would lose an
important part of their present function. Of course
there is a political choice involved. It is perfectly possible either to continue with the present
system or to change the BTn and BT into something
closer to the general baccalauréat so that they
would be viewed exclusively as a first step in the
process of higher education. Since in fact only a

The Lycée

Table 3.1
Table of subjects available in the first year of the
lycée and the number of hours per week for each.

Core subjects

French	5hr
History and geography	4hr
Modern language	3hr
Mathematics	4hr
Physical science	3½hr
Natural science	2hr
Physical education	2hr

Obligatory options

Either one of the following:

Industrial technology	11hr
Laboratory-based science and technology	11hr
Medical and social science	11hr
Craft	11hr

Or Economics and social science 2hr
plus one of the following:

Greek	3hr
Latin	3hr
Second modern language	3hr
Office management	5hr
Technology	3hr
Art	4hr
Music	4hr
Advanced sport	3hr

(An extra two hours is added to any of the ancient
or modern languages if they have not been studied
previously)

Non-obligatory options

Pupils may choose extra options from the second
group of obligatory options or from the following:

Third modern language	3hr
Art or music	2hr
Introduction to family and society	1hr
Typing (for those not having chosen Office Management)	2hr
Technical education	2hr

minority of those with a BTn find employment directly, in time it has to be complemented by further
study.
        Twenty-four BT and one BTn already do not share
the core subject timetable because early specialisation is demanded.(13) Examples of the BT include
those training in furniture making, in glass products for the building trade and as graphics tech-
nicians. The exception among the BTn is the one
for those wishing to specialise in music or dance.
Pupils who choose these courses therefore enter
what is called a 'specific' first-year class.
        But if those baccalauréats that demand specific
knowledge and skills exert a strong influence over
the whole of the three-year course, the influence on
the early course options of even the more general
baccalauréat is only somewhat less evident. Pupils
must be wary in their choice of first-year courses
since in order to sit certain baccalauréats (indeed
in order to get into certain second-year classes),
they must have already followed certain options. In
short, there is still a minefield to be negotiated.
At least the minefield is pointed out to them for
example in the publications of ONISEP but other
influences, not printed in the official brochures,
are at work in the lycées and these are at least as
influential in deciding pupils on their options.

Baccalauréat sections and reform

The baccalauréat is divided into eight major sections
known by the first eight letters of the alphabet.
The general baccalauréats are the following (the
brackets indicate their major specialism): A (literature), B (economics and social sciences), C (mathematics and physics), D (mathematics and natural
science), E (mathematics and technology). The BTn
are: F (various technical and vocational sections),
G (economics), H (information science). Some of
these are further sub-divided as we shall see later.
When it is realised that all the baccalauréats and
their sub-divisions differ from one another in their
exact mix of subjects and time spent on them, it is
little wonder that outsiders (and insiders too) rely
not so much on detailed brochures put out by ONISEP
each year but upon the bush telegraph. The message
that has been drummed out for many years is that
mathematics is king. This is because those who
study mathematics will have the greatest number of
higher education options and of prestigious outlets.
The section of the baccalauréat with the greatest

time spent on mathematics is C (nine hours per week in the final year) and this therefore heads the hierarchy. In fact E happens to have nine hours too but to this is added a crushing eleven hours of technology plus twelve hours of other subjects per week. Little wonder that E is thought to be a tough section and does not approach the popularity of C. Moreover it is tarred with the brush of technology.

Table 3.2 lists the <u>baccalauréat</u> sections and the number of pupils taking them at various times throughout the Fifth Republic.(14) Between 1960 and 1970 the average number of pupils taking the <u>baccalauréat</u> grew by over eleven per cent per year though subsequently it has slowed down. Since 1970 the number opting for A has fallen regularly and since 1976 the number has been lower than that taking D.

Table 3.2

	1960	1970	1980	1983
A	23,334	64,502	40,391	45,108
B	191	11,304	31,521	39,287
C	17,061	21,443	32,658	31,566
D	15,443	36,011	48,545	51,505
E	3,248	5,447	5,823	5,960
F	-	11,081	26,612	30,043
G	-	17,465	35,605	43,054
H	-	54	443	701

The literary section A still provides the majority of university entrants but university is second-best in France; the <u>grandes écoles</u> have more prestige and C provides by far the greatest percentage of pupils to sit their competitive examinations. But if many pupils wish to study in section C, it does not mean that most are allowed to. The law of supply and demand operates. The teachers of section C tend to demand higher marks, particularly in mathematics of course. B and D are therefore often the compromise options of the middle class since they do

at least contain a fair measure of mathematics. It
goes without saying that the children of the highest
socio-economic groups dominate C.

The popularity of C led over the years to a <u>de
facto</u> filtering function for it. That is, mathematics began to assume a disproportionate importance
in the decisions about pupils' future education.
Pupils and their parents have felt that they must at
all costs do a course in which mathematics features
strongly. Not all pupils however have had the
interest or capability and have suffered as a consequence of the increasing abstraction of the advanced mathematics syllabus. Moreover it became essential to opt immediately on entry into the <u>lycée</u> for
the C classes because, although in theory pupils
could transfer between sections if they found their
first-year course unsuitable, in practice any movement between the C section and the others became one
way - out - as the weaker fell by the wayside. The
greater amount of time spent on mathematics in the
first year effectively excluded later transfer to C.

This was the major reason for the creation of
the new first-year class, the <u>seconde de détermin-
ation</u> by the reform in 1980. It was an attempt to
delay early specialisation. The common core of
subjects with everyone studying mathematics for an
equal number of hours per week at least loosened the
iron grip. Apart from the technical options which
do still divide pupils in a major way, most first-
year pupils in the <u>lycée</u> now follow a timetable that
is much more common to them all than it was in 1980.
Roughly speaking (and still excluding the BTn) only
for fifteen per cent of their time would pupils be
doing something different from their peers. How
have the 1980 reforms fared so far? Before assessing
their effect, it would be as well to remind ourselves
why they were instituted.

Their intention was two-fold: firstly to allow
the <u>lycée</u> pupil a better chance of selecting courses
that squared with his interests and abilities and
not to make an irreversible choice too early;
secondly, to achieve a better balance between the
different <u>baccalauréat</u> sections. In essence this
brings us back to the attempt to free the system of
the excessive influence of C.(15) As might have
been expected, the reforms have had a mixed effect.

They were a logical major development of the
movement already clear in the reforms of the mid-
sixties and although they brought about a major
change in school organisation, they were hardly
radical and certainly not revolutionary. Thus those

84

parts of the system that are unaltered continue to exert the same sort of influence as before. The most obvious example of this is the existence of the specific section in the first year (though in fact this affects only a small minority) and the heavily timetabled technical section which must be chosen by those wishing to sit this type of baccalauréat. Paradoxically the latter is a potential source of weakness for the BTn since, although it gives those pupils who take this section in the first year the opportunity for opting out and switching to other sections thereafter, it precludes other pupils from opting in because they will not have spent sufficient time on subjects in that area. But besides the BT and the BTn, most of the general baccalauréats demand that certain subjects be chosen among the options in the first year, or indeed in the collège. For example those who wish to take section G in the second year must have studied English; to take Al (French-mathematics), A3 (French-art), B (economics) pupils need a second language.

But any reform has to contend with entrenched attitudes as well as entrenched organisational features and of the two the former is more difficult to change. As we have seen, the C section attracted the greatest numbers of able candidates as is evidenced for example by its having the highest percentage of passes at the baccalauréat. The abolition of the first-year C option and the postponing of the section until the final year of the course was designed to weaken the position of mathematics. Moreover by the simple procedure of most pupils being obliged to follow an identical first year, the classes should all be mixed-ability. In fact just as the collèges have often successfully circumvented the true mixed-ability class decreed by Haby, so the lycées have surreptitiously continued to maintain a hierarchy among the first-year classes. Lycées were faced with having to adopt criteria in order to divide into classes the total number of first-year pupils and the solution often found was to use the pupils' choice of first foreign language. At first sight, there seems little subversive about this, but there was more to it than meets the eye. German is generally considered to be the most difficult of the modern languages usually taught in schools and is thus shunned by the less able. A further refinement was to use pupils' principal option. Once again there is a tendency for certain options to be taken by the weaker (office management) or stronger (Latin) pupils and before long the old hierarchical

system had more or less re-established itself.
The reforms have brought other unforeseen
difficulties. Pupils who would have chosen a first-
year C because they were good mathematicians found
that the mathematics syllabus designed for the whole
of the intake was relatively easy. Unfortunately
for them the level of mathematics expected for the
examination at the end of the third year remained
the same. Consequently the second year became
hectic. This might well prove to be a temporary
difficulty only since the official line is that the
same level as before should not be expected of pupils
in their second year. It has tended to be teachers
themselves who have insisted on covering the same
ground as in previous years. Perhaps time will
effect a change here.
It is difficult for all attitudes to change
however if several of the premises upon which they
are founded still persist. Thus a C <u>baccalauréat</u>
continues to offer the most certain way of pursuing
the higher education course of one's choice. This
applies not only to courses in mathematics but also
many for which in theory the other <u>baccalauréat</u>
sections are preparing pupils. Thus investigations
at the universities of Caen and Montpellier have
discovered that although twice as many students with
the biology <u>baccalauréat</u> D than with C sit the first-
year examinations in medicine, only half as many
pass. Twice as many students with the economics
<u>baccalauréat</u> B sat the first part of the degree
course in economics as those with C yet thirteen
per cent of the former passed against 46 per cent of
the latter.(16)
Lest it be thought that the 1980 reforms can be
dismissed as a failure, let it be said that they
have also had beneficial effects. Many <u>lycées</u>
appear to have entered into the spirit of the reform
and not chosen to reconstitute the old divisions.
To some extent too pupils are beginning to choose
options more out of interest than just cold calcul-
ation. For example those studying for the BTn are
becoming more likely to try something like a second
language.(17)

<u>Traditional criticism</u>
Just as important as the detail of the reform is the
fact that the French administrative authorities
keep trying to improve the system. Although the
flow of instructions can be bewildering, it is the
expression of a desire to attack the shortcomings.

The Lycée

It would be churlish to complain that the 1980
reforms have not transformed the system, the fact is
that the Ministry of Education is constantly review-
ing practice and frequently modifying it too.
Unfortunately mathematics for example remains king
(bordering on dictator) but its hold has to some
extent been weakened. There is a will to get things
right. Of course there is room for discussion about
the strength of that will. The very existence of
the baccalauréat has been called into question for
years past. Besides the various criticisms already
examined which amount to a denial of the persistent
belief among the general public that it is a qualification which offers the same chances to all, the
baccalauréat is thought to be too complicated and
costly. It has also been accused of being a national obsession. Certainly media coverage is usually
extensive. By dominating the work in the lycée, it
overshadows everything that is happening there.
This of course has various undesirable effects. An
excessive interest in examination results frequently
leads to considerable pressure upon pupils which
would not necessarily be a bad thing if they were
afforded other outlets and if the pressure were not
so constant. However, clubs or sport or reasonable
teacher-pupil relationships have tended to suffer
and the comparison between the lycée and a factory
is often made. Teaching methods have also concentrated on the transmission of the syllabuses which
since they are usually very full have often been
rather uncompromising and frequently border upon the
lecture. Working under constant examination
pressure also prejudices the balance between the
subject itself and its examination. As the importance of the latter increases so the love of the
subject decreases and it becomes a mere means to an
end. In other words, education ceases.

All this affects the way the subjects themselves
are regarded. Their importance in the eyes of pupils
and parents (and often teachers) varies in direct
proportion to the number of marks they carry in the
examinations, some counting more towards the final
mark than others. Upon this latter point, it would
be difficult to find a satisfactory solution since
it is inevitable that pupils will value a subject
more highly if their future depends upon it. The
baccalauréat does after all retain its traditional
strength of offering a variety of subjects to pupils
until they reach adulthood.

As an examination the baccalauréat has also
attracted frequent criticism for the way it disrupts

The Lycée

the final term. The examination traditionally takes place in June and it is not unusual for lycées to close down completely as soon as the baccalauréat begins. Evidently the first and second-year courses also end. Even if a school does not close completely disruption to all lessons can be serious from the beginning of June since it is part of a teacher's conditions of service to mark examination papers. Schools therefore often try to allow for this by releasing markers to get on with their seasonal work and thereby arrange things so that they can begin their holidays at the same time as those not called upon to do any marking that year. The examining itself is unpopular among teachers who, not unnaturally, regard it as a supplementary chore. Strangely enough, many of those chosen as examiners are struck down by illness in the summer term since medical certificates are produced aplenty exempting them from these duties.

The most serious consequence of the baccalauréat being in June is the loss of school days. It is commonplace to hear that the school year in France is very short but in fact, as the Prost Report points out(18), the school year itself is not that much different from that in other European countries and neither is the length of the school holidays. What affects the lycée badly are those factors which eat into the normal school year. Many lycées try to keep Saturday free of as many lessons as possible since this allows those pupils boarding at school, some fifteen per cent of the total in general and technical lycées and twenty per cent in LEPs, to go home for a whole weekend. By not using the school on Saturdays, Heads are able to save on the cost of such items as meals and heating and so more easily stay within their budget. Unfortunately, Saturday mornings are judged as being available by those who write the syllabuses - not unreasonably since it is still an official school day. But if Saturday is not used, pressure builds up on the other days. (Wednesday is usually a free day).

The school year is further curtailed by a month because virtually no lessons are taught in June. Besides the influence of the baccalauréat examinations in that month, schools hold their final conseil de classe. These decide which courses the pupils will be doing the following year, based upon what they have achieved in the current year. Since nothing that happens after the meeting of the conseils will influence this decision, there is little point in doing anything after (or so the

The <u>Lycée</u>

Cartesian logic runs).

The Prost Report, by taking these factors into account, calculates that <u>lycée</u> pupils might be working only 155 days a year, which it calls 'derisory'. (19) It suggests various administrative improvements and recommends that all examinations should be taken in July as should the review of pupils' work in the <u>conseil de classe</u> since in effect only about ten per cent of the cases discussed are not straightforward. Attempts have been made in the past to regulate an aberration which has become the norm. Only time will tell whether more radical measures will be taken...and followed.

But complaints about the misuse of time by <u>lycées</u> do not stop there. The organisation of the school day has often been called into question. The basic unit is the hour-long lesson, often reduced by a few minutes to allow pupils to go from one class to another. This has been judged too short for practical lessons and too long for the type of chalk and talk teaching frequent in <u>lycées</u>. Be that as it may, many <u>lycées</u> pack them together without any other break in a morning or afternoon session than the time it takes to walk to the next lesson. This inexorable succession of lessons ignores the fact that people work better with an occasional break. Commerce and industry know this only too well.

If the school year and school day could be better organised, so too could the school week. It is impossible to be exact about the number of hours per week that <u>lycée</u> pupils work since this depends upon the type of course they are following, their choice of options and which year of the course they are in. Nevertheless since the weekly number of hours for each element is laid down nationally some rough idea can be obtained. Pupils following the general <u>baccalauréat</u> have some 30 hours of classwork per week, those following the BTn 36. Those studying for the CAP and BEP 32. Of course pupils are at school for longer than this since, for example, a good number take the midday meal at school. To many courses (particularly the non-technical) time may be added for homework, revision and so forth. Moreover, despite long-standing criticism of such weekly totals, the burden of work has got heavier not lighter in recent years.(20) It is little wonder that time-tablers find it impossible to give pupils a balanced week. One of a pupil's days might contain seven hours of lessons, another none.

The grip of the syllabuses is an uncomfortably tight one. The solution is simple: lessen the

number of hours. This apparently obvious way forward however brings one into a minefield. The difficulty lies in choosing which hours to drop. The
teachers of technical subjects maintain that any
loss of time will weaken the credibility of any
qualification with a practical component, whilst no
teacher of a non-technical one will admit his specialism is less important than any other. Ministers
of Education have changed the weekly content of the
baccalauréat repeatedly over the years but it is a
thankless task since it is not an exercise likely to
satisfy many; changing the number of hours in one
subject has repercussions for others. There is a
case for radical reassessment of the baccalauréat
content which for example might bring a truer
marriage of technology and the rest.

The Lycée d'Enseignement Professionnel (LEP)

The LEP is exclusively concerned with the vocational
training of teenagers. The studies leading to
either a CAP or a BEP are, like those for the BTn, a
mixture of strictly vocational courses and a general
education consisting of some easily recognised
subjects such as French and history. The fact that
students go to an LEP for vocational training and
thus specialise from the very beginning makes it
virtually impossible for them to change courses
after the first term. The qualifications gained
over two or three years are those which are univers-
ally recognised by employers. Because vocational
training begins at once it is impossible for all LEP
students to follow a common first-year course of
studies. There would undoubtedly be opposition from
employers to any such change which would parallel
that in other types of lycée since it would be
regarded as an adulteration of a student's training
and the employers would feel that they would have to
suffer the consequences. Moreover it would be
doubtful if any such move to bring the LEP courses
more into line with those in the other types of
lycée would receive much backing from anyone else.
Certainly it would be little appreciated by the
pupils. Training for a specific job provides the
major motivation for many of them. Indeed general
courses as a rule are regarded as of - not to put
too fine a point on it - secondary importance. If
such a subject as English retains a certain status
among those training for work in an office because
of its kudos with employers, for the majority of
pupils who are hoping to work in the industrial

sector it is often thought a waste of time. Periods
of their courses spent actually on the factory floor
or in an office (a practice considerably increased
since 1979) may not make the students' eyes sparkle
in anticipation, but at least they are practical and
therefore of some relevance to the majority. A
teacher of non-vocational subjects in an LEP often
has to work harder than colleagues teaching practical
courses.

Being at the bottom of the technical education
ladder also has its problems. We have already seen
in the previous chapter how the system of <u>orientation</u>
or the placing of pupils on courses appropriate to
their ability and interests tended to direct the less
able out of the mainstream of the <u>collège</u> and <u>lycée</u>
<u>général</u>. The LEP is where they often end up. Thus
it has more than its share of students whose education so far has not been marked by conspicuous
achievement. However, a fresh start on a different
type of course can bring about a change for the
better in a student's attitude. In addition the LEP
is more often than not an institution with less than
600 students and therefore is sometimes able to
create a feeling, if not of intimacy, at least of
belonging, something which is frequently absent from
the other types of larger <u>lycée</u>.

Nevertheless pupils already branded as academic
failures do not make the most promising material.
What makes teachers' tasks more difficult is the
fact that many pupils are not training for jobs of
their first choice. There exists the possibility
that no course dealing with their preferred subject
is available in their area, and students must reckon
with being offered a place on a course which is their
second or third choice. Various factors govern the
allocation of places and the most important among
these is past academic performance. Inevitably some
courses, say in the catering or tourist industries,
are more sought after than others and so competition
is stiff. Students also have to contend with the
possibility of not finding a job when they become
qualified. The benevolent eye of central or regional
education officials is employed to adjust supply to
demand but such fine tuning of qualified personnel
to jobs available is beyond the capacity of any
administrative machinery yet devised in a democracy.
It therefore happens that although demand is high
for certain courses, these are often the very ones
in which there is no corresponding social demand.

LEPs sometimes also suffer from their relatively
low status. They often need considerable investment

in their equipment and its maintenance and financial
stringency has greater potential deleterious consequences for a course which depends upon machinery
than the traditional chalk and talk course does.
Not surprisingly, money is spent in preference upon
such things as lathes or typewriters rather than
exterior paintwork with the consequence that LEP
buildings are sometimes unattractive.(21)
    Such brakes on motivation contribute to the
fact that about twenty per cent of pupils used to
abandon their studies. Since 1980 the figure has
dropped to something like fifteen per cent no doubt
because of the increased fear of unemployment.(22)
About six in ten students pass the final examinations. Employment or unemployment (both fudged
together in many Ministry of Education documents
under the title vie active) is not the only outlet
for LEP pupils. For a small percentage of the best
a few lycées techniques have classes which prepare
them for entry into a BT or BTn course. Such students usually need to be eighteen and have a modern
language and this type of further study is not available at the end of all LEP courses.

Courses
The course in the LEP with the most sections is the
CAP. This trains students to be cooks, electricians,
mechanics and so forth. Large firms do provide some
training facilities but, as has already been said,
it falls principally to the state to provide the
country's skilled work force. The CAP theoretically
should cover all skilled jobs but in fact LEPs have
never managed to do this. Extensive though these
courses are, doubts have been raised in the past
about their suitability in a modern state. It was
during the 1960s that fears grew that excessive
reliance upon the CAP might hinder rather than help
the development of French industry, for although
these courses are adapted to meet different circumstances, and indeed new ones are regularly created
and old ones closed, it was felt that the CAP had
become too job-specific. In an effort to introduce
flexibility into a final qualification the BEP was
created. There are now some 50 BEP which aim to
straddle several jobs and thus make the qualified
person more easily adaptable to the changing needs
of industry. The BEP are divided into three broad
areas: industrial; commercial and administrative;
health, social and catering. Thus, for example,
a BEP in the health studies sector might lead to a

para-medical career or to nursing (after further appropriate training); someone with a BEP in the social sector might work in establishments catering for children, teenagers or old people.

The idea originally was for the BEP to replace the CAP but the latter enjoyed such currency and confidence among employers (and their opposition to such a move was so strong) that the idea was dropped. Indeed the BEP has taken some time to convince employers in the industrial sector that it can provide them with workers of sufficient expertise, though employers in other sectors have been more easily won over.

There is one other qualification obtainable in the LEP and this is the CEP (<u>Certificat d'éducation professionnelle</u>). This is very much the poor relation. It is designed for those students unable to take a CAP or BEP and lasts one year. Thus its students are either those who are incapable of following the (already modest) intellectual content of the longer courses or who do not choose to undertake longer study. There is no examination for the CEP and it is awarded on the basis of course work. It is hoped that the CEP will act as a springboard to the CAP since its level of qualification is only just above that of the unskilled worker. The creation of such a course once depended(23) upon a local need being identified for the products of some appropriate slant to the CEP but these terms have had to be made less strict in the face of rising unemployment. Less than 10,000 students follow CEP courses as against some 450,000 for the CAP and over 300,000 for the BEP.

Apprenticeship Centres

The CAP (and CEP) can be prepared not only in an LEP but also in an apprenticeship training centre (<u>Centre de formation d'apprentis</u> or CFA). The most important education-apprenticeship link before the Fifth Republic was forged by the so-called Astier Law just after the First World War. Its first major modification came in 1971 when the CFA was created. Those doing apprenticeships must now register with the CFA and thereby commit themselves to a minimum of 360 hours work per year in one in addition to the time spent in a firm. These establishments are unevenly distributed throughout France since they tend to be located in areas which have a tradition of a certain kind of apprenticeship. The centres supply the theoretical input for the CAP whereas the employer

guarantees the apprentice the practical training.
How an individual firm and the local CFA allocate
the time necessary for the training of an apprentice
depends upon local conditions but apprenticeships
usually last two years (sometimes extending to three,
for example in the printing trade) with the apprentice going to the CFA one week in four. Apprenticeships are granted to girls as well as boys, the one
condition being that the candidates must be between
the ages of sixteen and twenty. Moreover they must
register with a CFA which of course allows the state
to ensure the various responsibilities undertaken by
both sides are kept. This does however often amount
to a theoretical supervision only since the number
of inspectors doing this work is insufficient to
examine anything like all cases. One final remark
on this system of training should be made and that
is that the CFA cater for those areas of training
that demand the less advanced skills. For example,
the young men attached to these centres gravitate
mostly towards the building, mechanical and food
trades rather than, say, the electronics industry.

Unemployment

It was during the 1970s that France along with other
Western industrialised countries experienced unprec-
edented levels of unemployment. The world recession
with the consequent reduction in industrial output
and the constant striving for competitiveness by
firms competing on the world market not only threw
many out of work but also prevented many school
leavers from finding employment. In France, as elsewhere, it was this latter section of the population
that was most acutely affected. This has had its
consequences for the school system and not least
among such has been the increase in malaise especially among those pupils with few or no qualifications since these are the most likely statistically
to suffer. Another effect has been the increasing
preference among pupils and students for vocationally
orientated courses. In the higher education sector
for instance medical studies become ever more prized
since they offer the twin lures of status and money
for those who qualify. But at a lower level the CAP
has attracted those who a few years previously would
have spurned it either for higher level studies or,
more particularly, for a (then attainable) quick
entry into the world of work. The latter type of
pupil now realises that there is no longer likely
to be a job for those who quit school at the first

opportunity. Qualifications therefore have increased in value but such an increase has not been uniform. The CAP, for example, can still be a passport to a job but some of these qualifications are more valuable than others. Thus the textile industry, particularly hard hit in recent years, no longer absorbs those who take their CAP in that subject area. The holder of the G option in the baccalauréat (secretarial studies) has often found that further qualifications have been needed if a job was to be obtained.

Government reaction to youth unemployment has been reasonably consistent especially since the mid-seventies. Various schemes have been introduced to prevent young people from feeling excluded from a society which is unable to offer them adequate employment opportunities. In 1977 Raymond Barre, the Prime Minister (and former professor of economics), launched the PNE (Pactes nationaux pour l'emploi), a scheme which offered tax incentives to firms willing to take on youngsters under 26 years of age (for a limited period). Within the next year or so the PNE had a considerable impact on the unemployment figures since about a quarter of a million young people enrolled and a further 200,000 joined firms for practical courses.(24) In fact it has been shown(25) that the great majority of those helped by the PNE already possessed a qualification and were over eighteen years of age. In other words, the PNE did not help those in greatest trouble: the unqualified. The government of François Mitterrand attempted to remedy this. The minister then in charge of vocational training, Marcel Rigout, helped set up between 1982 and 1984 some 800 centres called either PAIO or missions locales(26) largely run by organisations experienced in social work of various kinds. Here youngsters were given vocational guidance and efforts were made to raise their level of education either by setting up remedial courses in such areas as mathematics and language or by attempting to re-integrate youngsters into the school system or by encouraging firms by tax incentives to offer some sort of training to youngsters.

In fact the education service gave only lukewarm support to the efforts of the PAIO in that the various types of work experience did not fit easily into the structure of the usual state qualifications such as the CAP. Neither was a system of exemptions elaborated which might have enabled some youngsters to use their experience to begin a recognised course. Cooperation was often difficult to achieve between

the various organisations which were unused to acting together. These included schools, local authorities and government employment or training organisations such as the ANPE and the AFPA.(27)

By the autumn of 1984 the socialist government
was multiplying such schemes - largely derided by
the Opposition - and placing increasing responsibility upon local authorities to come up with the cash
for them. One such, the TUC(28), supported small-
scale enterprises and individuals if they supplied
services not covered by the usual agencies within
the local authority areas. Part financed centrally
and part locally, this scheme has proved quite
popular with youngsters reluctant to return to
school.

Such schemes are palliatives of course and
their application is not always appreciated by those
elements of society which see their vital interests
threatened. For example, the education service has
not taken to its bosom those pupils who only recently
failed in the system and small service firms often
see the state and local authority financial support
for such schemes as introducing unfair competition.
Nevertheless the justified retort would be that in
the circumstances something is better than nothing.

From the grime-covered LEP in an industrial
suburb of Paris to a spanking new showpiece in a
residential area of Lyon, the French lycée is represented by a wide range of institutions. Their defects
are many but these are no more numerous than in
similar institutions in other countries and at least
they retain a good deal of public confidence. The
lycées - particularly those doing courses leading
to the baccalauréat - dispense what is considered to
be the best education available. No one believes
that a better academic education can be obtained outside the state system. This does not prevent parents
from thinking that one lycée is better than another
and various devices for getting their offspring into
the one of their choice are employed by those in the
know. Equality may be in the state's motto and it
may make an attempt at even-handedness in the distrib
ution of funds and teachers but forces conspire
against it. There is nothing fundamental the state
can do about the relative attractions to the better
teachers, say, of the town and country or the north
and south. Nevertheless the education system is
almost always a central concern of French governments and the lycée like the collège has always

96

attracted attention. Lycée teachers are more likely
to complain of change than stagnation and the pace
of change has probably accelerated in recent years.

NOTES

    1.   Also sometimes known as the Lycée classique
et moderne.
    2.   'Technique' can be translated only roughly
by 'technical' which in English has strong industrial
overtones. In the French education system it covers
courses etc. which are concerned with the acquisition
of a certain expertise needed for a particular job.
I have used the word 'technical' therefore in a
broader sense to include all sectors, not only the
industrial one.
    3.   Décret du 28 déc. 1976.
    4.   Les Lycées et leurs études au seuil du XXI
siècle, Ministère de l'Education nationale, Déc.1983,
p.175.
    5.   John Ardagh, France in the Eighties, p.480.
    6.   See the circulaire du 15 fév. 1977 for a
description of the responsibilities of the professeur
technique chef des travaux (PTCT) to give him his
full title.
    7.   This is one of the criticisms voiced by
Georges Pompidou when Prime Minister. See the report
upon a parliamentary debate in Le Monde, 21 mai 1965.
    8.   The baccalauréats F,G and H.
    9.   Education, 17 juin, 1971.
    10.   H.Jeanblanc, Organisation de l'enseignement
en France: le second cycle, Univ. Lyon II, CDRP 1975.
    11.   For a history of this sector see A.Léon,
Histoire de l'éducation technique, Que sais-je?
PUF 1968.
    12.   In 1958-9 there were some 58,000 pupils
following the 'long' technical courses. By 1982-3
there were some 285,000. The 'short' course numbers
in those years rose from some 220,000 to 630,000.
    13.   In all (in 1985) there are 26 baccalauréat
sections: A1,A2,A3,B,C,D (and D1 for agriculture),
E,F1,F2,F3,F4,F5,F6,F7,F7bis,F8,F9,F10(A),F10(B),F11,
F12,G1,G2,G3,H. The number of hours per week demanded by these courses can be seen from an illustrative
appendix.
    14.   Ministère de l'Education nationale,
Repères, p.199.
    15.   See the press conference given on 10 Nov.
1980 by Jean Saurel, the head of the lycée section
at the Ministry of Education.

16.   Statistics gathered by the CUIO (Cellules d'information et d'orientation) between 1978 and 1982 at Caen and 1982-3 at Montpellier. Quoted in *Le Monde de l'éducation*, fév. 1984.

17.   Service académique d'information et d'orientation de Nantes, *Orientation des élèves de seconde* (1981-2).

18.   *Les Lycées et leurs études*, p.107.

19.   Op. cit. p.108.

20.   Op. cit. p.106.

21.   For such an unfortunate case see 'Un LEP en détresse', *Le Nouvel Observateur*, 28 juin, 1983.

22.   Lucien Geminard, *Le Système scolaire*, p.29.

23.   Circulaire du 10 juillet, 1969.

24.   These and the following figures in this section are to be found in 'Emploi des jeunes: du social à l'économique', *Le Monde de l'éducation*, juin, 1984.

25.   José Rose, 'L'incidence des pactes nationaux pour l'emploi sur l'insertion professionnelle'. *Education Permanente*, juin, 1980.

26.   The PAIO or *permanences d'accueil d'information et d'orientation* numbered 700 and were run by one or two people. The *missions locales* numbered 86, were staffed by more people and enjoyed major support from local authorities who had in fact to request that they be set up in their area. Sixty of the eighty were in areas controlled by left-wing councils

27.   *Agence nationale pour l'emploi* and *Association pour la formation professionnelle des adultes*.

28.   *Travaux d'utilité collective*.

Chapter 4

HIGHER EDUCATION (1)

After the baccalauréat there are basically four
higher education routes open to French students.
The first takes them through a higher class in a
lycée; the second through a grande école; the third
through higher technological studies; the fourth
through university.

Lycées
A French lycée can span the divide between secondary
and higher education when some of its pupils undertake a course leading to the qualification of brevet
de technicien supérieur(BTS) or one that prepares
its students for the competitive examinations that
have to be sat for entry into the grandes écoles.
Thus, although young men and women pursue their
studies in a school, they cease being pupils and
become students and indeed are entitled to enjoy the
same privileges as those at university. For example,
they are entitled to the subsidised meals obtainable
at a university restaurant and may be eligible for a
state grant.
      Not all lycées however belong both to the
secondary and higher education sectors. Only a
minority run the two higher types of course. Indeed,
since each type is further subdivided, this minority
of schools tend to specialise and teach only part of
each course. The sort of specialist teaching
required in these higher education sections ensures
that all such lycées are to be found in large towns,
though Paris dominates the scene by virtue of the
range and number of courses on offer. The relative
scarcity of this higher provision confers greater
status - particularly in the case of the preparatory
classes - upon these lycées (thereby enhancing the
reputation of Paris as a centre of excellence) and

also obliges many students desirous of following
this route either to travel considerable distances
or to board. Moreover only the brightest are
admitted. Yet there is no shortage of applicants.

The higher technical sections or STS(1) contain
students wishing for a specialist qualification
usually in the tertiary sector of the economy.
Courses last two years after the baccalauréat in a
technical lycée and if the student is successful in
his final examination, he has the option of going
straight into employment since the BTS is vocationally orientated or of continuing his education
either at a grande école or a university. However,
the BTS enjoys a good reputation among employers
and so most students get a job.

More prestigious and a good deal better known
is the second kind of higher education available in
certain lycées: the preparatory classes for the
grandes écoles (classes préparatoires des grandes
écoles or CPGE). These are exactly what they sound
like - classes for those students who wish to prepare for those grandes écoles that organise competitive examinations for entry. They contrast with
the STS in that they do not lead to a terminal
qualification - and are thus not designed to equip
their students to enter the world of work. As might
be expected from a type of education with such a
specific target in mind, the divisions within it
correspond closely to the sort of grande école being
aimed at. There are five types. First, the scientific classes within which mathematics predominates
(though some have technological options); second,
there are those specialising in biology and agriculture; third, veterinary sciences; fourth, business
studies and fifth, there are the literary classes.
As we shall see later, the grandes écoles offer an
enormous range of subject options but clearly they
cannot be reflected exactly in the lycées, hence the
match between preparatory classes and grandes écoles
is only a broad one - though the classes are further
subdivided in some cases.

Traditionally the preparatory classes only
admitted students with a baccalauréat from one of
the series A,B,C or D but since 1978 the BTn has also
become acceptable. Nevertheless, as we saw in the
previous chapter, the most successful baccalauréat
section for entry into the preparatory classes is C.
About 40 per cent of its pupils manage to get a
place in the preparatory classes, followed by E with
about a 30 per cent success rate. Only about seven
per cent of the literary section of the baccalauréat

enter these classes. To some extent of course this
reflects the fact that the brightest pupils opt for
mathematics but the fact that far more places are
available in the grandes écoles for those who have
studied mathematics also reinforces the importance
of selecting the right baccalauréat sections.(2)

Life for the student in the preparatory classes
is renowned as an unremitting slog under considerable
pressure. The Ministry of Education warns pupils
thinking of taking this route that: 'These classes
expect a higher than average level of achievement
plus intensive, regular and methodical work. The
syllabuses demand a speedy assimilation of their
contents. Only pupils capable of sustained, prolong-
ed effort, physical as well as intellectual, enjoying good health and being well balanced can attain
their goal.'(3) Despite such warnings, pupils know
that their best chance of a highly paid job lies in
pursuing their studies in a preparatory class. That
is primarily why the numbers in these sections have
grown so rapidly as the table(4) below illustrates:

	1960-1	1970-1	1980-1	1982-3
CPGE and STS	29,052	59,441	106,672	120,527

Many fall by the wayside and many fail to secure a
coveted place at the end of the day. For these
students there always remains the university. Indeed
when they enter the preparatory class they are advised to register at the local university as a form
of insurance. Since student fees at French universities are nominal this is a simple matter. So too
is their ability to pass the university examinations
at the end of the first and second years since the
teaching they receive at the lycée incorporates
frequent monitoring in a hot-house atmosphere which
contrasts with the leisurely impersonal one at
university. Such a system obviously tends to devalue
a university education in the eyes of the French but
at least the preparatory class failures can continue
their studies and obtain a degree. Life may be hard
in the preparatory classes but their status is high.
The teaching received there is recognised as being
of a higher standard than in any other part of the
higher education system. Students are not only made
to work hard but are also taught how to work hard,
something the university for example usually ignores.
The success of the preparatory classes is implicitly

101

recognised in the 1984 reform of the higher educational system (to which we shall return later)
wherein it was proposed to set up preparatory classes
in universities as one way of improving students'
job prospects. Presumably however it would take
some time before the reputation of these new preparatory classes becomes as great as that of those in
the lycées. But if French universities suffer by
comparison with one sector more than any other it is
that of the grandes écoles.

The present organisation of higher education studies
Before dealing in more detail with the various parts
of the higher education sector, it is as well to
outline the composition of studies in the grandes
écoles and universities.
    Studies in an IUT (Institut universitaire de
technologie) last two years including some two
months' work experience attached to a firm and leading to the DUT (Diplôme universitaire de technologie).
    University courses in law, economics, business
studies, humanities and science are divided into
three stages or cycles each lasting two years. The
first cycle can normally be undertaken only by those
with the baccalauréat and successful completion of
which leads to the award of the DEUG (Diplôme
d'études universitaires générales). As the name
implies, this is a general diploma and might be made
up of course units from different disciplines.
Students may seek employment with the DEUG, though
it has no great appeal to employers. Efforts are
being made however (as we shall see later) to
improve its image. Students may repeat only one of
the two years if they fail it. The DEUG allows its
holder to proceed to the second cycle. After one
year students may obtain a degree (licence) and
after a further year's study a master's degree
(maîtrise). The alternative route offered by the
second cycle is to enter immediately upon a course
leading directly to a master's degree. These are
vocationally orientated higher degrees: the
maîtrises de sciences et techniques(MST), maîtrises
de sciences de gestion(MSG) and the maîtrises de
méthodes informatiques appliquées à la gestion
(MIAGE). The second of the two routes however
accommodates only a restricted entry and competition
is strong. In consequence the majority of students
pass via a two-stage cycle - though they may of
course leave with a first degree and not proceed to
the maîtrise. A master's degree is however the

requirement for continuing into the third cycle.
The studies undertaken here vary in length. Normally students wishing to proceed to a doctorate
would first do a DEA or Diplôme d'études approfondies
which lasts a year. Lasting the same length of time
is the DESS (Diplôme d'études supérieures spécial-
isées) which is the third cycle vocational qualification. In addition some MST can lead on to a
Diplôme d'ingénieur and then (intercalating the
DEA) to the Diplôme de docteur ingénieur(DDI).
Finally studies in political science, available in
seven specialised Institutes, demand that the student pass an entrance examination or some other form
of selection. These studies last three years.
     The various medical studies differ somewhat
from the rest and between themselves. Those wishing
to become doctors are trained over a minimum period
of seven years. The first cycle lasts two years
though there is a competitive examination at the
end of the first year, the number of places available
in the second year being calculated according to the
need for doctors - as perceived by the Ministry of
Education and the Ministry of Health. Most students
fail. The second cycle lasts four years during
which periods are spent working in hospitals. The
third cycle leads to the Diplôme d'état de docteur
en médecine. This is variable in length depending
upon a student's final area of specialism. This
cycle was reformed for the year 1983-4 in order to
come more into line with the rest of Europe. Now
the students have four possible options: general
medicine, public health, medical research or specialised medicine. The first three of these last two
years though only the first is open to all students.
Entrance to the others depends upon the results of a
competitive examination. The last option offers a
range of specialisms from surgery to psychiatry and
lasts four or five years. Those students who will
become dentists share the first year of their course
with those who will become doctors and so sit the
same examination as them in order to go into the
second year. Dental studies last five years in all
and lead to the Diplôme d'état de docteur en
chirurgie dentaire. It is possible to continue into
the third cycle which is exclusively concerned with
research and which leads to various qualifications.
Studies in pharmacy follow the same pattern as those
for dental surgery with a competitive examination
at the end of the first year.
     The grandes écoles are very varied in the
courses they offer but they usually last three or

four years (excluding any time previously spent in preparatory classes on order to gain entrance) and lead to various diplomas. It is to this sector we first turn.

The grandes écoles

It is difficult to characterise with any precision the considerable range of subjects taught in the grandes écoles. The simplest procedure is to link them up with the broad area of administration or industry for which they train their students but even this is not foolproof since some grandes écoles do not aim to find their charges jobs in specific areas. Many moreover teach several specialisms. Nevertheless they do tend to emphasise an expertise in one professional concern rather than another thereby allowing a loose division to be made.

The first category and the most famous is that of the écoles d'ingénieurs. It is misleading to call them engineering schools for they do not train what English speakers think of as engineers. Even if we were to ignore such complications as an engineer possibly being a garage mechanic or (in America) a train driver and remained with a definition of someone of graduate status with specialised knowledge in an applied practical field such as mechanical or chemical engineering, the translation of ingénieur by engineer would remain inappropriate. The French ingénieur is usually someone trained as an executive, often within a reasonably specialised field. According to the Commission des titres d'ingénieur, the body with the task of validating courses and qualifications, there are 153 such schools(5) which can be divided into thirteen categories according to their specialisms. Since little detail is usually given in English sources on the grandes écoles, an example of an institution in each category has been included in brackets. The categories are as follows: agronomy (the INSA - Institut national des sciences appliquées - at Toulouse); defence and aeronautics (the Ecole spéciale militaire de St Cyr at Coëtquidan); physics and chemistry (the ENS - Ecole nationale supérieure - de chimie at Mulhouse); electronics (the ENS de l'électronique et de ses applications - at Clergy); energy (the Institut francais du froid industriel - in Paris); civil engineering (the ENS d'hydraulique at Grenoble); computer science (the Institut d'informatique d'entreprise at the Conservatoire nationale des arts et metiers - in Paris); mechanics

(the ENS de méchanique et des micro-techniques - at
Besançon); geography (the Institut de physique du
globe - at Strasbourg); textiles (the Institut
textile de France - at Boulogne); wood, leather,
paper (the Ecole française de tannerie - at Lyon);
health (the Ecole nationale de la santé publique -
at Rennes). The final group specialises in not
specialising or in offering a considerable range of
specialisms such as the Ecole centrale at Lyon or the
Institut catholique d'arts et metiers at Lille.

The grande école can be either state or private-
ly owned though they virtually all come under the
aegis of government departments. Naturally the
Ministry of Education oversees the functioning of
the great majority - two thirds of them - but the
Ministry of Agriculture is responsible for over
twenty and the Ministry of Defence for about a dozen.
The rest are divided between the Post Office, the
city of Paris and the Ministries of the Environment,
of Transport, of Health and of Industry.

The next largest group of grandes écoles are
those specialising in commerce and business studies.
It is virtually impossible to categorise these
closely and they often differ between themselves
about the emphasis they place on the various sub-
divisions that go to make up their studies. Moreover
this is a category of grande école that has no
validating body like the écoles d'ingénieurs and has
a particularly strong tradition of private involvement. This is not very surprising since most owe
their creation to a sector of the economy (always
having had a great number of private owners) in which
individuals or groups of private citizens have sought
to satisfy a need they felt for highly trained managers either in their particular sector of activity
or in their particular part of the country. Many of
these business schools are closely linked to local
Chambers of Commerce. Examples of these are the
Ecole des hautes études commerciales in Paris and the
Ecoles supérieures de commerce in various towns such
as Le Havre, Marseille or Bordeaux.

Another group is that which trains students for
careers in architecture most of which deliver a
state qualification. The majority are organised in
what are called architecture training units (Unités
pédagogiques d'architecture or UPA). Most of these
are in the Paris area. Other types of organisation
exist however such as the private Ecole spéciale
d'architecture(ESA).

A fourth category of grande école is that providing courses to train top executives mostly in the

Civil Service and in which administration and law
feature prominently.(6) Catered for in this group
is a considerable range of activities and included
here are such institutions as the Ecole nationale
de la magistrature and the five Instituts régionaux
d'administration. Included here too are the écoles
normales supérieures whose products originally
entered the education sector. These have recently
been completely reorganised. The four comprise
the amalgamation of the one at Sevres and the rue
d'Ulm (in Paris), the ENS de Fontenay-Saint-Cloud,
(again merging the two former ENS), the ENS de
Cachan which replaces the technical grande école and
the fourth is to be the ENS de Lyon, an entirely
new institution being built in the centre of that
city and due to have its first intake in 1987.

The fifth and final group of grandes écoles
must be labelled miscellaneous. They include those
institutions that train people for the Merchant Navy
or to be veterinary surgeons or for careers in the
arts and newspaper world or as translators.

It is rather difficult to obtain precise statistics on the number of students enrolled in the
various grandes écoles though the statistical branch
of the Ministry divides them in two: the écoles
d'ingénieurs and the écoles de commerce. Whatever
way they are divided there is no doubt that their
popularity has grown steadily as the following
table(7) indicates:

Student Numbers

	1960-1	1970-1	1980-1	1982-3
Ecoles d'ingénieurs	20,770	30,512	36,952	39,000
Ecoles de commerce	5,286	9,394	17,730	23,317

France's grandes écoles enjoy the high status
conferred by competitive entry and good job prospects. They are regarded as pinnacles of the
higher education system. Yet there is enormous
diversity between them, even greater diversity than
between universities. The grandes écoles that
immediately come to the mind of the average Frenchman are such institutions as the Ecole Polytechnique
or the Ecole nationale d'administration(ENA). But
there are some 300 grandes écoles and inevitably

with such a large number standards vary. In fact,
there is no official definition of what exactly
constitutes a grande école. Perhaps this is hardly
surprising since from the sixteenth century onwards
individual schools have been created in response to
particular professional needs.

It is the motivation behind their creation
which points to what is perhaps their most salient
characteristic: their links with the professional
world. The grandes écoles have grown up by fulfill-
ing society's needs for professional training as
they have arisen. Some of the best-known examples
of this occurred during the Revolutionary and Napoleonic periods when the state needed, for example,
army officers (which led to the creation of the
Ecole Polytechnique) and teachers for the lycées
(écoles normales supérieures) but only a handful of
specialised schools were created then. It was as
the French state became more complex in its organisation and commerce and industry developed apace that
the écoles proliferated. Now there is hardly an
area of the modern state that does not have its
corresponding grande école. But if the grande école
is professionally orientated, its products are all
expected to enter management positions since the
qualifications are of (at the very least) degree
standard.

Once again the universities have suffered in
comparison. Indeed it was their inability to adapt
to changing conditions that led the government or
private individuals or groups to think of creating
the grandes écoles to satisfy its needs in the first
place rather than to try modifying the universities.
Attitudes in this matter began to change under the
Fifth Republic as we shall see later but the universities have a long way to go to reach the level of
cooperation that exists between the grandes écoles
and the country's higher reaches of administration
and industry. The universities entered this game
relatively late. Apart from the medical and legal
faculties, the university did not begin to train the
graduates for managerial positions until the 1950s
and this has hampered their efforts to become accepted, especially by French employers, as real altern-
atives to the grandes écoles. The latter have always
had the reputation of being able to adapt rapidly
to what was needed by employers whereas universities
have always been viewed as ivory towers. Even today when several universities have been in the business of producing post-graduates especially qualified
in areas of direct relevance to commerce, industry

and administration, employers still prefer the products of the grandes écoles.(8)

It is this link with industry and commerce which reinforces the dynamic image of the grandes écoles and which they of course do what they can to foster, especially since they compete between themselves for students. It is the business schools in particular that have proved adaptable. As the pressure of international competition between business concerns has grown more intense, so these ESCAE (Ecoles supérieures de commerce et d'administration des entreprises(9)) have had to respond to change. Outside France it is often thought a truism that the central administration in Paris must provide the initiative for most things in that country but in fact the private sector can often hold its own. For example it was as recently as 1984 that the ESCAE in Grenoble opened its doors for the first time despite the fact that there was already one in nearby Lyon and that the city already had several higher education institutions including two which had close ties with the business world.(10) Local firms supported its creation because they felt there existed a gap in the training received in such institutions. It was recognised that products of most business schools go straight into top administration whereas many felt there was a lack of marketing executives able to work on the home market and all over the world. The emphasis in the ESCAE in Grenoble is therefore upon selling industrial products - something that the French often complain they could be better at. The concentration upon international marketing quickly won the sponsors of the new school, the Chamber of Commerce in Grenoble, support from both local and central government and the ESCAE was rapidly set up in new buildings in the town. The grande école is also a good example of how such institutions can be integrated into existing structures. It relies for some of its teaching upon the staff of the town's école d'ingénieurs, the INPG (Institut national polytechnique de Grenoble) and upon the rich variety of technically advanced industry in the Rhone-Alpes region.

Grandes écoles make strenuous efforts to involve executives in their work. They are regularly brought in to help run courses and their places of work are used to give students periods of on-the-job training. The grandes écoles have been quick to seize further opportunities to strengthen such links. The passing of laws in July 1971 to encourage the development of continuing education and - just as

important for the competitive grandes écoles - the
allocation of money to those institutions prepared
to organise such courses was soon seen as an opportunity to expand their activities. Most grandes
écoles thus provide opportunities for managers wishing to undertake refresher courses or to acquire new
knowledge and skills.

Not all grandes écoles enjoy a good reputation
for the level of their teaching however. Some of
the most prestigious have only a small permanent
staff and, whereas a certain influx of temporary
staff can have its advantages, it can also have disadvantages such as lack of coordination and continuity. Posts in the grandes écoles are not necessarily popular with university staff either since
attachment to them can cut off lecturers from research and thereby hamper their careers. Neither is
it unknown for students who have worked unremittingly
for perhaps the two years before entering a grande
école to take the opportunity, once they have
secured a place, to sit back and wait for a diploma
which will guarantee a good job. Very few fail the
courses.

Hardly any grandes écoles contain more than
1,000 students and most have between 100 and 500.
Part of the explanation for the adaptability dis-
played by these institutions is thought to reside in
their relatively small size. The theory is that
this has enhanced their likelihood to adapt to
social conditions. This belief is so pervasive that
when the universities have set up courses parallel
to those run in the grandes écoles they have always
been keen to keep down the size of these new departments.

One final factor that distinguishes the grandes
écoles from the universities is the highly selective
nature of their intakes. As we have seen, many of
the grandes écoles demand an intensive two-year
period of preparation for those wishing to sit the
entrance examinations. But this is not true for them
all. Some take students after a single year's preparatory course whilst others take them straight
after the baccalauréat. Some choose students on
their school record.

The basic justification for stiff entry qualifications has always been that, in a Republic that
boasts of equality as a fundamental principle, all
candidates are chosen according to their merit and
not, as in the bad old days, according to which
family they came from or how rich they were. Nevertheless the most prestigious grandes écoles in part-

icular have produced elites. This is something
which most people in France find perfectly natural.
Indeed this is the very reason the schools were set
up. However fewer people find it acceptable that
the sons (rarely daughters) of this elite gain a
disproportionate number of places in these schools.
It is of course a well-established sociological
phenomenon that a country's upper social groups do
better than others in an education system. The Left
in France has felt concerned about this. Indeed it
was one of the few Communists in the Mauroy cabinet
under Mitterrand who made a dent in what he regarded
as the elitist vicious circle. Anicet Le Pors, the
Secretary of State for the Civil Service, changed
the entrance requirements for ENA, the State's most
prestigious training ground for top civil servants,
soon after being appointed to his post in 1981. Le
Pors believed that the background of France's top
men should reflect the composition of society. The
intake of ENA might for example include only twenty
per cent of students from the lower social categories
which in fact composed forty per cent of the working
population. The solution adopted was to reserve a
certain number of places for people working in a
wide range of jobs. In addition, instead of being
placed in order of merit at the end of the course
and allocated jobs according to their position as is
the custom, the new breed of candidate would be
classed on their own separate list. Various organisations were invited to put forward candidates'
names. Although employers' organisations were
included, the initial response was strongest from
the trade unions and in particular from the Communist
led CGT (Confédération générale de travail). Some
right-wing politicians have viewed this change as
little less than an attempt by the Left to keep a
firm grip on power but it is difficult to see how
this can be achieved, even if that was the inspiration behind the change. It seems likely that this
revolution will be quietly absorbed, especially if
candidates of quality keep coming forward.(11)
       According to other left-wing opinion, such
changes amount only to tinkering with a system
which should be dismantled and merged with the universities. When the Socialist Minister of Education
Alain Savary was preparing a new law to reform the
higher education sector, this was one of the proposals that was considered. Here at last was an
opportunity to break the power of France's elites
and to give the country one unified system. The
grandes écoles however, despite their image of

exclusiveness, are generally regarded as having served France well and Savary who only had to look around him in the upper echelons of his own party to see that it was not only the Right that was benefiting from such a system, rejected any such fundamental change. His new law, as we shall see later, was to affect the universities much more than the grandes écoles and indeed this reform was partly inspired by the latter's success.

The Instituts universitaires de technologie (IUT)

The third part of the higher education sector is formed by the Instituts universitaires de technologie (IUT). These are officially attached to universities, each IUT being counted as a separate department. However, they are often treated apart and indeed the length and content of their courses differ markedly from those in the other departments which make up the university and so they will be dealt with as a discrete element before we come to the rest of the university sector.

The IUT are the latest addition to the French higher education system. They were created in 1966 under Christian Fouchet to meet a long-felt need(12) for people trained to promote the French economy and to fill the gap between those trained by the secondary schools and the écoles d'ingenieurs. The IUT began life with a possible eighteen different departments and a government review of the sector in 1983 confirmed that they should continue with this number. No single IUT offers this range, a typical number of departments being six. Apart from the departments of computer science, they are divided broadly between those termed industrial and those termed tertiary each corresponding of course to those sectors of the national economy. The industrial departments consist of such subjects as applied biology, chemistry and industrial maintenance; the tertiary of such as business and administrative management, social careers and information services (see table 4.3). Many departments have a range of options though individual IUT do not create their own courses since they can only offer options created by the Ministry of Education. Thus in applied biology, the subject with the largest number of options, an IUT could only offer one or more of: agronomy, biological and biochemical analysis, food technology, nutrition or environmental management. Like the higher classes in the lycées and the grandes écoles, the IUT select their students. It

Table 4.3

A list of IUT studies

Applied biology	Information Science
Chemistry	Legal Studies
Chemical Engineering	Social Careers
Civil Engineering	Health and Security
Heating Engineering	Quantitive Management
Industrial Maintenance	Marketing Techniques
Technical Measurement	Transport Studies
	Business and Administration Management

is not sufficient simply to be in possession of the baccalauréat, a student's (good) school record is the key to a place. In addition there is an interview. In theory the number of students admitted to an IUT depends upon the demand within the economy for the type of training chosen but of course other factors enter the calculations such as the availability of staff and equipment. The courses at an IUT last two years and at the end is delivered the DUT. This can be obtained in one year by students who have the university diploma awarded after the two-year first cycle studies. The DUT is a terminal qualification in the sense that it can lead straight into employment though approximately twenty per cent of those in the industrial departments and thirty per cent of those in the tertiary ones go on to gain further qualifications often by undertaking degree-level studies at university. It is not unusual for pupils to opt for the IUT rather than the university since it does offer a diploma after two years' study which can be immediately used. Moreover the courses at the IUT are more intensive than at university and are closely supervised. Students at the IUT can expect to be working 30 to 35 hours per week in lectures, seminars and so forth. Demand for places in the IUT far exceeds supply though the system of multiple applications between IUT and other institutions of higher education means that the IUT, like universities, harbour (sometimes disgruntled) students who failed to gain a place in a grande école.

Government intervention in the IUT is patent. The director is appointed by the Minister of Education and since the French government has a history (pre-dating the Fifth Republic) of being directly

involved in economic planning, the regulation of the
IUT output is seen as of immediate national concern.
Recently the future development of this sector has
been linked with the Ninth Plan. Thus for example
in 1983 new computer science departments were
created in the IUT in Metz and Dijon, management
studies in Corte and micro-computer technology
courses were added to chemistry departments. Such
areas as electronics and robotics were being boosted
by concentrating government money to promote them.
Just how closely the government views its involvement in this sector can be judged by the fact that
it was President Mitterrand himself who announced in
April 1983 that places in the advanced technological
departments would be doubled between 1983 and 1988.
Expansion in IUT numbers has already been fairly
rapid. By the end of 1966, the year of their
creation, there were thirteen IUT, now there are 66
with about 55,000 students.

Besides the obvious national economic need,
local political influence has also sometimes been at
work here. Towns and regions have felt that the
presence of an IUT conferred status and have fought
hard for one to be sited within their jurisdiction,
even if at times the local economy did not always
merit it. Pascale Gruson(13) wondered if the IUT at
Rodez, for example, with only a single department
could be strong enough to be considered a full member of the higher education system.

Another difficulty associated with the IUT has
been the shortage of full-time staff. A large
number of courses are taught by part-time or temporary staff and although the socialist government did
initially spend money on the creation of more full-
time posts, there remains a considerable shortfall.
Moreover, as with the grandes écoles, qualified
personnel are often reluctant to be appointed to IUT
since they have traditionally been restricted to a
teaching role only whilst many lecturers see their
chances of advancement coming through their contrib-
ution to research.

The Universities

The final and largest sector in the higher education
system is that of the universities(14). Table 4.4
illustrates the growth in university numbers in each
major area. Generally regarded as cumbersome and
slow to adapt, in fact they have not been immune to
some change. The law degree, already reformed in
1954, continued to be reorganised in the first

Table 4.4

	1960-1	1970-1	1980-1	1982-3
Law and economy	36,521	149,340	191,384	199,789
Arts	66,814	233,605	262,665	286,637
Science	71,102	111,544	132,271	142,772
Medical Studies	40,235	136,162	188,802	188,074

couple of years of the Fifth Republic. Economics was introduced as part of the degree and this discipline was also instituted as a free-standing degree from 1960. In 1963 a preparatory year had been introduced for medical studies with places on the course being allocated according to the number available in teaching hospitals. As we have seen, technological education was also given a fillip with the creation of university technological institutes in 1966. The Minister largely responsible for this major development was Christian Fouchet who also reorganised the structure of degree studies in the mid-sixties.(15) The first cycle of university studies had previously lasted a year and had been followed by an examination which had to be passed in order to continue with the degree course. This was replaced by a two-year first cycle followed by a second cycle which led to a degree after one year and a master's degree - an entirely new qualification - after a further year. Theoretically the former degree was designed mainly for teachers, the latter for those wishing to do research and continue into the third cycle. This cycle led to a doctorate. This is the broad pattern which subsists to this day.

The sixties had also seen the setting up of several new universities to meet the growth in demand for higher education principally occasioned by the rise in the number of eighteen year olds. A science faculty was added to the University of Paris at Orsay and a faculty of letters at Nanterre. New universities were created in the provinces at Amiens, Nantes, Nice, Orleans-Tours, Rheims and Rouen. Many other universities had new campuses added usually on the outskirts of their particular city and extensions to universities were created in medium-sized towns like Chambéry and Pau.

These instances show that the university system had been adapted to changing circumstances.

Unfortunately it was not adapting fast enough. It is often said that too little was being done too late. Commentators were freely using the word crisis to describe the state of the university sector(16) and this crisis was to come to a head in the incredible events of 1968. The crucial cause of these was the increase in student numbers.

French universities have long admitted the largest proportion of those who wish to enter higher education. For many years the sole criterion for entry to university was the possession of the <u>bacc-alauréat</u> and indeed this with any combination of subjects more or less guaranteed a place in a faculty of a student's choice. The consequence of this semi-open access policy was that many more students enrolled for university courses than in those countries operating a <u>numerus clausus</u> system. Nevertheless the French policy offers a splendid opportunity for a wide range of secondary school pupils to try student life to see if it pleases them rather than slamming the door in their faces. Some students might well discover the motivation that was lacking in secondary school, especially if they began afresh with a new subject. Because the issue is seen as one of equal opportunity, many of those in the university, especially the students not surprisingly, have tended to support this argument. To most Frenchmen the counter claim that standards are threatened is not usually regarded as strong since the examinations sift out those who are not good enough to continue their courses. However, the university system tolerated rather than adapted well to the accommodation of large numbers of students. Students found it dispiriting to sit in a vast lecture theatre bulging with those who chose to attend. Indeed it was fortunate that most did not choose to attend lectures since there was not enough room for them all. The same could be said for such facilities as university libraries. W.D.Halls quotes Gerald Antoine, a former rector of the University, who in 1962 declared that the Sorbonne continued functioning only because half the students never went to lectures and 90 per cent never entered the libraries.(17) Of course many registered without intending to sit the examinations at all. Some, for example, paid the modest registration fee and thereby gained access to the subsidised university restaurants - a practice which continues to this day.(18)

All the various problems associated with overcrowding were exacerbated by the dramatic rise in student numbers in the sixties. They approximately

doubled to some half a million during that decade.
Just how great a transformation this brought about
can be gauged by the fact that by 1967 the higher
education sector had become the size that the secondary sector had been about a decade before.(19)
Discontent rumbled constantly in the background and
occasionally flared up in minor riots and demonstrations with numerous student arrests to catch the
headlines, as at the Sorbonne in February 1964.

The government was aware of the situation, and,
as we have seen, had responded by building new
universities and extending old ones. Moreover many
appointments were made to university staffs.(20)
Universities however remained soulless. Students
regarded them as little better than factories but
with no guarantee of obtaining a qualification with
much status on the job market. Lectures were over-
crowded and contact with lecturers virtually non-
existent. Indeed since many a lecturer sold copies
of his lecture notes, attendance on the course was
often unnecessary (provided one could pay for the
notes, which were not cheap). Grants were few and
far between and were in any case low. Many students
therefore had to work in order to pay for their books
and accommodation. Ideally they would find a post as
a surveillant in a secondary school which simply
entailed keeping an eye on pupils during their breaks
and in the dormitories in those schools with boarding
facilities. This sort of job at least gave long paid
holidays but inevitably studying was difficult and
failure rates were high. Universities offered virtually no social life, interests having to be pursued
outside it. The idea therefore of a community was
almost entirely absent. To make matters worse,
unemployment among graduates was rising as France
became unable to absorb the numbers being produced
by the universities. Various reforms were viewed
with a jaundiced eye by students. A majority accepted the system with resignation, a minority grew to
hate it.

Demonstrations like that in February 1968
against inter alia the right of political expression
in halls of residence were the affair of such a
minority. Over the years small groups of extreme
left-wing students had made most of the running in
student politics. However there was hardly any
cohesion among such groups and they were only
occasionally united as for example in violent clashes
with extreme right-wing groups. Certainly the famous
events that took place in May 1968 were not the outcome of some deep-laid plot by leftist militants,

though these did foment trouble when it broke out.
They exploited any opportunity to throw stones at
the police, for example, and pushed generally for a
break-up of the then existing university system (and
a very few even for a break-up of the state).
Earnest conversations at the time tended to concentrate on first the necessity of getting rid of what
existed. Only later would thought be given to what
would be put in its place. But the student revolt
could not have happened if the discontent of such
groups did not find some echo in the student body as
a whole. Eventually large numbers of students joined in demonstrations and even riots, not so much
because they found them exhilarating (which they did)
but because the various conditions already outlined
gave them genuine grievances and made them ready to
act. The huge majority of students at the time were
considerably less motivated politically than socially
however.

No doubt there were in addition more profound
reasons for discontent but enough has been written
about such matters for them to be passed over here(21);
nor is there any need to describe what happened in
1968 in any detail. Nevertheless since the incidents
of this period are unique not only for the education
sector but for the whole of France, they deserve to
be chronicled briefly in order to give some idea of
their extraordinary nature.

The most significant first step in the escalat-
ion of the events occurred at the new but desolate
faculty at Nanterre on the outskirts of Paris when
on the night of 22 March about 150 students occupied
the administrative offices on the campus. The date
is significant mainly because it gave a focus for
several leftist groups who thereafter took the name
of the 'Movement of 22 March'. The Dean ordered the
closure of the faculty on the 29 and 30 March though
demonstrations continued to break out occasionally
throughout the next month. The faculty was again
closed following the occupation by students of the
main lecture theatres at the beginning of May. The
situation rapidly deteriorated after 3 May when
students (many from Nanterre) who had gathered in
the centre of Paris to protest at the disciplining
of several colleagues for their actions at Nanterre
were ejected from the Sorbonne and many taken to
police stations in order to have their identity
papers checked. That night came the first clashes
between students and police. On 4 and 5 May the
police surrounded the Sorbonne and those arrested
during the riots were sent to prison by hastily

convened courts.

The two immediate causes of the considerable student involvement in the demonstrations - as their chants indicated - was the imprisonment of some of their comrades and the entry on to university premises of the police, albeit at the invitation of the Rector. During the evening and night of 6 May students rioted throughout the Latin Quarter and that night the unfortunate Minister of Education Alain Peyrefitte appeared on television to justify the closure of the Sorbonne and to appeal for calm. He was wasting his breath. The sealing off of the Sorbonne by the police acted like a red rag and after a march across Paris on 7 May, students once again rioted.

Although Nanterre was reopened (and immediately reoccupied by the students) on 10 May, the Sorbonne remained closed and once again rioting took place. If possible it was even more violent with dozens of barricades being thrown up around the Latin Quarter. The material for these was literally lying at the students' feet in the form of granite blocks used to cobble the roads. They also proved to be excellent ammunition to fling at the riot police.

The following day the Prime Minister Georges Pompidou returned from his visit to Afghanistan and immediately set about handing back the Sorbonne to the students and lecturers. The unreality of the times may be partly gauged by the fact that on 13 May, the tenth anniversary of De Gaulle's accession to power, a huge march organised by students' and lecturers' unions and the Movement of 22 March took place perfectly peacefully in Paris and De Gaulle himself flew off for a state visit to Rumania. The following day Pompidou announced that imprisoned students would be amnestied. No doubt he hoped that now that the two earlier student demands had been met, normality would return. If so, he hoped in vain. In fact matters got rapidly worse. The chaos in the Latin Quarter spread not only to secondary schools and other universities but to French industry as workers began occupying their factories. De Gaulle cut short his state visit on 18 May but within a few days France was in the grip of a general strike. The President appeared on television on 24 May in a conciliatory mood but rioting followed that night in many major cities. The government bent all its efforts to get people back to work but the agreements hammered out with the unions on 27 May were largely rejected by factory workers.

The beginning of the end came on 30 May when a

more peremptory De Gaulle announced on the radio
that he was dissolving Parliament and calling a
general election. Gradually things started going
the government's way. Factories began reopening and
police acted more decisively in their dealings with
students. Demonstrations in various parts of France
continued for some time into June but the general
election at the end of that month gave the supporters
of De Gaulle a massive majority. The new government
and the new Minister of Education Edgar Faure set
about reforming the universities.

University reform after 1968

Faure immediately began a process of consultation to
discover how best to reform the universities. The
outcome was the Loi d'orientation de l'enseignement
supérieur which was promulgated by the President in
November 1968. The students by their violent actions
had ensured that change had come suddenly. The
universities were completely reorganised. Yet in a
strange way the profound structural changes hardly
touched the immediate concerns of the majority of
demonstrating students: unemployment, soulless
institutions and a vague dissatisfaction with society.
The universities continued to turn out people qualified in areas which society found difficult to
absorb and few seemed to derive much more enjoyment
from the new courses than before. The students'
rallying cry of 'participation' by which was meant a
say in their own education was followed by positive
action in the new law. Students were to be represented on the various bodies of the new institutions.
By the following year about 53 per cent of the students nationwide voted for their representatives,
though from the beginning the consultation process
ran into trouble with the UNEF - the national
students' union - calling upon its members to
abstain. By 1970 only just over 30 per cent of
students bothered to vote in what was really the
first election in the newly created universities.
By then however they had come to realise being in a
minority on university bodies was not going to
change things as they might have hoped. Moreover
two years had passed since the events of May 1968
and the visible outcome of all that effort - a few
student representatives on university committees -
seemed like the proverbial mouse engendered by the
mountain. Disillusion was inevitable particularly
as neither the government nor the university did
much to publicise the change or to present the idea

of student representation as something that at
least could play its part in a more democratic
university structure. Indifference to the new measure grew apace and only those with definite political
leanings - usually left-wing - took the trouble to
stand for election. In turn this type of student
has not often proved attractive to the ordinary
student voter who frequently does not even bother to
vote. In fact the student expecting a real say in
the running of the university has good grounds for
complaint. It is still true that, although his representatives have a voice on the governing body of
the university, the University Council (Conseil
d'université), they have little influence. Not that
they are in any way unique since the Council, composed of a wide range of representatives, tends to
encourage factionalism. The powers of the Council
may be real enough, voting the budget for example,
but it is dominated by the university President. He
is the executive arm and alone possesses the necessary administrative back-up to run the university.
Among other things, he appoints to posts (from a list
drawn up by the Ministry), allocates responsibility
and cash, represents the university in all matters
and - a key responsibility - decides upon the agenda
of the Council and carries out its decisions. Thus
he is the only member of the Council sufficiently
well placed to provide continuity in the administration of the university. The Council is frequently
reduced to approving decisions made by him.

The 1968 Loi d'orientation was the most radical
restructuring of the university this century. Before
this date universities were hardly any more than a
collection of independent faculties which regulated
their own internal affairs with little reference to
each other or therefore to the university as a whole.
Students, for example, spoke of attending the faculty
not the university. In principle a university was
composed of five faculties: law, medicine, pharmacy,
letters and science, though many were composed of
fewer. This structure concentrated power in the
hands of the professors and the highest ranking
members of staff of the various faculties. If a
professor did not possess absolute power, he could
certainly demand (and obtain) a large degree of
conformity from staff since subordinates' careers
depended very much on him. Yet even a professor's
freedom was relative since the Ministry of Education
kept a close eye on what happened in each faculty.
Academic staff had complained for years about the
Ministry's interference in the running of the univ-

120

ersity. A conference called by them in Caen in 1966 to discuss French higher education outlined the various changes judged to be necessary. The faculty structure was felt to be stifling and a more part-icipatory democratic structure was demanded. Also desired was a more diversified system with inter-disciplinary courses, autonomy from the Ministry of Education and the possibility of obtaining private investment.

After 1968 things changed somewhat: the old faculties were broken up and the Ministry of Educ-ation loosened its grip. In the latter case a degree of financial autonomy was obtained by each university being given a general budget and being allowed some freedom by no longer having to obtain prior consent from the Ministry for expenditure. Before 1968 the university as such had no budget, the credits being allocated to faculties. Universities thus obtained a measure of autonomy - something they had long demanded. However such autonomy is not great. After all, universities still rely almost exclusive-ly upon funds supplied by the state; they have not succeeded in diversifying their sources of income and very little money comes from private investment. Moreover the money allocated to equipment is sub-jected to fairly tight Ministry control. The Min-istry can also suggest to the individual universities desirable ways to enter into agreements with outside bodies and how to spend the credits advanced.(22) But restrictions upon a university's financial free-dom are a good deal less stringent than those upon individual departments. Indeed these have no legal autonomy in law and depend upon the university Pres-ident for the allocation of funds.

The most easily perceived break with the past came with the splitting up of the old faculties into subject departments or UER (Unités d'enseignement et de recherche). These UER were supposed to ensure that their courses gave students the opportunity to combine disciplines much more easily than before. Article 6 of the new law stated that 'The universit-ies are multi-disciplinary and must associate as much as possible the arts and letters with science and technology'. This was an attempt not only to give a boost to studies across subject boundaries but also to break up institutions that had grown elephantine. The UER would recombine to form smaller universities. This was easier said than done. The first approved list of UER to become universities appeared soon enough (in May 1969) but concerned medium-sized towns like Amiens, Caen or

Limoges which could in any case be expected to have
one university only. It was in the larger towns
that the difficulties lay. Faculties, if they split
at all, divided not only into subject departments
but also parts of departments. Thus an English
department might break up into a section that concentrated upon literature, another upon civilisation
and another upon interpreting. In other words, a
town like Montpellier might have more than 30 UER
which had to group themselves into an unknown number
of universities. (In this case three emerged).
Furthermore the composition of universities did not
simply depend upon educational criteria. Political
considerations played their part. Faculties and
sections of faculties sometimes had definite political leanings and were therefore reluctant to associate with those of different persuasions. Law faculties, for example, tended to be right-wing and
social and political science sections left-wing.
Indeed during the May events (and before) it was not
uncommon for fighting to break out between students
of these particular faculties.
     De Gaulle had resigned in 1969 to be replaced
by Georges Pompidou. He in turn appointed Olivier
Guichard to oversee the final phase of the restructuring of the universities. Despite the various
obstacles, by the beginning of 1970 all the new
universities had been formed apart from those in
Bordeaux and Paris. However a gentle reminder from
the Minister ensured that by the end of the academic
year France had got its new university system.
Paris, the most elephantine of all, had been split
into thirteen universities, seven in the centre and
four on the outskirts (one on each major point of
the compass) and two experimental universities
(Dauphine and Vincennes) which aimed to admit mainly
mature students who did not necessarily have the
baccalauréat. By the early seventies France had 57
universities and six university centres.
     The 1968 law also allowed the universities to
develop modular degrees whereby students took various options which were self-contained but which
built up into a degree. Continuous assessment also
became much more widely accepted in the university
system.

University autonomy
We have seen how the possession of the baccalauréat
allowed secondary pupils to enter university and how
this system helped swell numbers. Some restrictions

had already been introduced before 1968 notably in the university institutes of technology which operated a <u>numerus clausus</u> system but, as Edgar Faure pointed out at the time, this was a development not encouraged by the 1968 law. Nevertheless a significant change was to come under Olivier Guichard in a new law of July 1971. henceforth medical students would sit a competitive examination at the end of their first year. The numbers permitted to pass would be determined nationally and would be linked directly to the number of places available in teaching hospitals. To have the state decide how many students it needs nationally without any reference to particular institutions of course reduces university autonomy. The issue of selection is always guaranteed to raise the temperature of students in particular but the governments in the 1970s tended to generalise the process to other studies by no longer basing the size of individual grants upon the number of students in it but allocating instead a block grant, thereby obliging the universities themselves to operate as best they could some form of selection.

Moreover the Ministry of Education followed the <u>loi d'orientation</u> by a series of directives which largely determined the form of degree studies. Thus the law degree, for example, had to contain certain obligatory courses and in practice this severely limited the number of options available no matter which university a student attended.

The state as guarantor of standards has not been the only factor limiting initiative of universities; they have also suffered from the arbitrary way UER came together. A particular casualty of this has been cross-disciplinary courses - ironically one of the objectives of the 1968 law. As we have seen, reciprocal mistrust often prevented certain UER coming together. This plus the need to have a university of a certain size (which meant the number of students it could enrol) did little to ensure that logic dominated the creation of the new universities. Their inspiration was in other words Rabelaisian not Cartesian. In consequence opportunities for multi-disciplinary study were probably reduced rather than increased since universities were often made up of parts of the former faculties. In addition, many a UER became introspective. One academic commented a few short years after the 1968 law had come into effect: 'The creation of multi-disciplinary universities corresponded certainly to a laudable impulse, but because of the way it was set up, never have we been so far from our colleagues in other faculties'.(23) Modular degrees offer the opportunity judiciously to combine complementary elements that were impossible under the old system. But this seems to have been a theoretical possibility, not achieved in practice.

The gap between theory and practice depends critically not so much upon the way an organisation is structured as upon the attitudes of those operating it. The relationship between the universities and the Ministry of Education under the presidency of Valéry Giscard d'Estaing from 1974 to 1981 is a good illustration of this.

The period began well enough with the appointment by the new Minister of State for the Universities Jean-Pierre Soisson of an ex-university President Jean-Louis Quermonne. This was viewed as a move to inaugurate an era of dialogue between Paris and the universities. Such incidents as the Minister's withdrawal of the validation of the sociology diplomas at the University of Poitiers as early as 1974 and his declaration that this university's examinations were a 'mascarade' did not fundamentally shake the belief of university staff in the new era since they regarded such intervention as normal. It was felt that the Minister had reasonable cause for this action since he had responded to a call to intervene from the university's President. At least he had acted as arbiter and most acknowledged that he was doing nothing less than his duty. Indeed it could be said that he had acted more reasonably than his predecessors at the Ministry of Education. Olivier Guichard, for example, had done the same thing for the philosophy degree at Paris VIII-Vincennes in 1970 and had overruled the decision in 1972 of the University of Paris VII-Jussieu and its President to recruit someone to a temporary post. It is true that the person in question was Alain Geismar, one of the leading lights in the events of 1968, but Guichard was clearly politically rather than educationally motivated by his intervention. All this illustrates the importance of taking into account the cultural context of such words as dialogue. In any case even in its restricted sense, dialogue did not last long. Vigorous action returned with a vengeance with the appointment to Soisson's post of Alice Saunier-Séité in January 1976.

For the remainder of Giscard's period in office, the universities had to deal with an outspoken Minister with an autocratic bent. In the year of her appointment her style is captured in the early declaration that 'firmness is necessary' in order to prevent 'develop in the universities this general attitude of irresponsibility and indifference which abandons power to organised and active minorities'. (24) Anything that smacked of the Left and what was termed a 'lax' attitude (they were often synonymous in her eyes) were pounced upon. The University of Nanterre, hotbed of opposition in 1968, was regarded by the Minister with special suspicion and its law department soon came under threat of being closed. Saunier-Séité's new firm line was applied just as soon in the case of the University of Pau which had some of its examinations cancelled by the Recteur of Bordeaux. As we shall see in a later chapter, the Recteur is responsible for the education service in the whole of each education region or académie and acts on behalf of the Ministry of Education. Such developments obviously dismayed Quermonne at the Ministry of Education and, as Saunier-Séité ensured that the major decisions for the higher education sector were increasingly taken by her cabinet or personally appointed advisors, he resigned in 1976.

The university sector as a whole did not remain quiescent. In 1978 the university Presidents con-demned Saunier-Séité's unilateral changing of the conditions of employment of the junior lecturers (assistants) and the Minister's announcement in the same year of her intention to move the new university of Vincennes to St Denis roused considerable oppos-ition. As we have seen, Vincennes had been some-thing of a pioneer in the post-1968 period by, for example, accepting students without the baccalauréat but it had always been too extreme for the tastes of successive Ministers. In 1977 Saunier-Séité had openly accused it (in one of those remarks that were the delight of the press) of being a den of drug-pushers. The right of Vincennes to stay on its original campus was widely defended but petitions signed by the likes of Jean-Paul Sartre would pres-umably have done little to mollify the Minister. Nevertheless pressure from the universities did cause her to make the lecturers' conditions of employment somewhat more favourable - though Vincennes was eventually moved (with the help of the police) to St Denis.

The general thrust of the policies carried out by Saunier-Séité were of course approved by Giscard. Occasionally he intervened in an effort to reduce the tension caused as, for example, in 1976 when

the Secretary of State threatened to withdraw validation for certain degrees, but on the whole the
President was happy to support her. Evidence of
this is provided by her promotion from Secretary of
State to the head of a fully fledged Ministry for
the Universities in January 1978. (This was reintegrated into the Ministry of Education in 1981
though shortly afterwards a sort of compromise was
effected when the university sector was given its
own Secretary of State once again). The creation of
a separate Ministry was regarded at the time with
some misgivings rather than delight by the universities. The apprehension felt by academics was justified. Various alterations were made to the organisation of the universities in mid-August 1979.
Such a time, in the dead heart of the university
vacations, was a ploy (not entirely unknown outside
France) to introduce measures with a minimum of
reaction from an institution that would be largely
empty at that time of year. One change was for the
power of appointment of higher grades of staff to be
withdrawn from the Conseil d'université in each establishment. Admittedly, any such choice had had to
be made from the Ministry-approved list but soon
staff were to be allocated by a national committee.
The previous year the Recteurs, direct government
appointees, had been given the power to decide
whether or not to renew the contracts of junior
lecturers in their region. Another change ushered
in during the 1979 summer vacation was a measure to
give professors (a university grade, not necessarily
a position of responsibility) an absolute majority
on the university governing body. The other grades
of university staff, assistants and maîtres-assist-
ants had been recruited in large numbers during the
sixties and had taught an increasing percentage of
the courses which gave them a large measure of
representation on university committees. The professors had often disliked this trend and many had
withdrawn from governing bodies which in turn increased the influence of the other two grades. There
seemed to be little to object to on this point in
the new regulations therefore since the professors
tended to hold the more responsible positions in a
department and they had a right to be represented
but it was seen by many as a move to reinstate the
mandarinat or absolute rule of the professors as it
had existed before the 1968 reforms. Feelings ran
high and not just among the lower grades of lecturer.
For example, Michel Denis, the President of the new
University of Haute-Bretagne, resigned over the issue.

It was in July 1980 that Saunier-Séité was to stir up even greater opposition with the announcement (affecting most universities) that dozens of courses would not be validated the following year. The decision was taken against the advice of the body officially designated to give it on university matters, the CNESER(25), and soon university Presidents as well as staff and student unions and opposition parties were up in arms. Even the RPR, one of the two important political parties making up the government, joined in the protests. The Minister defended her action as a means of rationalising courses in an effort to lessen wastage and to attack poor standards(26) but a direct appeal to the Prime Minister Raymond Barre by the university Presidents led to an eventual reprieve in September for many threatened courses. Whether Barre intervened for educational or political reasons is a moot point.

Reform in the eighties

If Edgar Faure's higher education law in 1968 was the first major change to the university system in the Fifth Republic, that of Alain Savary was the second. Many of those in the university sector however who had expected the universities to be among the first institutions that would be altered by the left-wing government in 1981 were disappointed that it had not happened during the initial flush of reforming zeal that infused the new government's first few months in office. At the congress of the left-wing university teachers' union, the SNE-Sup(27), held in June 1982 to discuss what changes should take place, many delegates expressed surprise that nothing had yet happened. They had however only a short time to wait. In the following October the Minister outlined his new law inspired, he claimed, by its famous predecessor. The delay had been caused not by a lack of interest in the university question but by a protracted system of consultation undertaken by the Ministry of Education. A commission had been set up in November 1981 under Claude Jeantet in order to prepare a report upon which this new law could be based. Opinions and evidence were canvassed from a wide range of political parties, unions and organisations in the social, economic and educational fields. Considering the university sector's reputation for sensitivity, it must have been heartening for the Minister when the proposals were made public that reaction was at least mixed and not wholly hostile.

The proposals themselves aimed to be more wide-ranging than the 1968 law. Savary intended the new law to take in all institutions of higher education and indeed they were all to be brought under the umbrella title: établissements publics à caractère scientifique, culturel et professionnel. The attempt to view the diverse higher education system as a whole was novel. In reality however the gap between theory and practice remained wide since that part of the higher education system principally affected by the new law was once again the university sector.

The law itself reads strangely. Article 12 blithely states that 'the provisions relating to the placing of students in institutions and on courses precludes any selection' but is immediately followed by the words: 'However, selection may be operated according to procedures fixed by the Ministry of Education for entry to...' and then comes a list which includes the preparatory classes for the grandes écoles, the grandes écoles themselves, and the IUT. The formation of elites was judged too necessary to modify.

The 68 articles that eventually emerged contain several key alterations to the then current practice. The first of importance was the affirmation that any pupil with the baccalauréat or an equivalent qualification could enter higher education. At first sight, there seemed little radical about this since the French system had long prided itself upon its semi-open access policy. But again theory had long not been followed in practice. Inevitably some universities and some courses were more popular than others and they had often evolved their own individual methods of solving the problems associated with supply and demand. Ultimately each had the safeguard of quite simply calling a halt to the registration of students when their courses were full. In Paris, for example, the most popular universities are those in the centre of the city, the less popular on the outskirts. The tradition had thus grown up of queues of prospective students forming early in the morning on the first day of registration. It was simply a matter of first come first served. If a student was unfortunate enough to be too far down the queue to be included in that university's quota, he had to take himself off quickly to his second-choice university and hope the queue was not too long there. It remains far from unusual for students to register for a course different from the one originally intended so that they might at least gain a place.

But universities had instituted more precise methods of quality control. Some departments insisted on a particular type of baccalauréat (often C), others judging by a student's school record, others (though rarely) by an interview. Fairly common among selection procedures was the insistance upon a distinction being obtained in the baccalauréat. When the socialist government abolished the award of distinctions some departments started taking into account the actual percentages gained by individuals. Thus arose a veritable semi-official jungle of requirements. The new law forbade selection. It also extended a student's choice by enabling him to apply to any university in the country whereas before he was supposed to apply to one within his académie if the course he wanted was available there.

Two major reasons underpinned the government's reaffirmation of the semi-open access policy to the universities. Firstly, it was done in the names of democracy and justice. It was considered wrong that a student who had attained a certain educational level should be excluded from at least trying to go further. In other words, secondary school studies should not be a determinant for the pursuance of higher educational studies. Secondly, a large proportion of the country's young people in higher education was seen as a guarantee of the nation's future economic strength. Claude Jeantet for example had viewed with concern the drop in the percentage of 20-24 year olds in full-time education. In this matter France had fallen from third to seventh position among the OECD countries.(28) This is rarely questioned in France and assumes the importance of an article of faith and appears in the introduction to the 1984 law:

> The access of a larger number to higher education will not only make possible a greater future guarantee to each citizen of equality of opportunity. It will also give to the country, by the increase in the general educational level and the training of an ever-increasing human resource from which to recruit the most inventive minds, the conditions for the development of the country's knowledge and technology and therefore its economy.(29)

However it was one thing to allow easier access to higher education and thereby increase the number of students, it was another to ensure that the time was

well spent and that these studies led to employment.
Savary was only too well aware of the fact that
almost half of those who entered university left
during the first two-year cycle of studies without
any qualifications whatsoever. His analysis of the
situation led him to the view that premature specialisation by students in the first cycle caused a loss
of motivation and contributed to the drop-out rate.
He therefore proposed that the first-cycle studies
should allow more leeway to students before they had
to specialise. This was to bring down upon his head
the wrath of some factions of the universities and
we shall return to this a little later.

A less controversial suggestion for the first
cycle was a greater emphasis upon the personal
guidance of students in efficient working methods.
The traditional style of teaching had hardly changed
over the years despite the bitter complaints voiced
in 1968: crowded lecture theatres leavened by the
occasional and only slightly less impersonal seminar.
The feeling still persisted that the student was
very much on his own. If he failed, it was nothing
to do with the university staff, he simply had not
worked hard enough. Savary looked to the <u>classes
préparatoires</u> for inspiration in this area for, if
they had the deserved reputation for being forcing
houses, they also had one for carefully monitoring
students' progress. Moreover the form of first-
cycle studies desired had been the subject of some
teaching experiments at various universities. One
conducted at the new University of Grenoble in
1982-3 provided a pointer for the future. A group
of 160 students was split into five groups of 32.
The large-scale lecture was abandoned in favour of
seminars and certain remedial courses were laid on
for those needing to bring their knowledge up to
par. About twelve per cent more students than
usual succeeded at the end of the year. What they
liked about the experiment were the small groups and
the type of teaching this made possible as well as
the improvement in relationships generally. They
also liked the greater number of lecturers involved
and the closer monitoring of their work.(30) Any
change in this direction was therefore unlikely to
meet any opposition from the students. They did
object however to one other - far more novel - aspect
of Savary's proposals.

This was the greater emphasis to be placed in
the first cycle of university studies upon professional training. In future many courses were supposed
to reflect the world of work and new courses were to

be instituted which were specifically professionally
orientated. Such a move (which was also to affect
second cycle studies) went under the name of professionalisation and was mainly aimed at the large
number of students who did not intend going beyond
the first cycle. In the past the DEUG had little
or no currency on the job market since it was intended exclusively as a preparation for second-cycle
studies. Henceforth it was to be designed to stand
on its own and to have prepared students so that
they might more easily obtain employment within
broad sectors of the economy. As part of this
strategy preparatory classes for the grandes écoles
were to be established in universities. The first-
cycle diploma was in other words the higher education
equivalent of the BEP.

Savary's suggestions would thus appear to be
good news for students but if he had hoped that the
earliest mildly favourable reactions would last, he
was to be disappointed. Opposition to some of the
proposals gradually gathered momentum and in the van
of this opposition were the country's university
medical and legal departments. Students, urged on
by staff, took part in demonstrations because they
objected to the postponement of specialisation. The
broadening of the first stage of medical and legal
studies was largely viewed as a waste of time by
those students who had in any case opted for specialised studies from the outset. By delaying specialisation they feared (and their professors confirmed)
that this would mean that their courses would have
to be lengthened in order for the basic work usually
done at the beginning of the courses to be covered.
A certain edge was lent to the (eventually) more
generalised protests of these university departments
by the fact that they traditionally contained a
higher than average proportion of right-wing sympath-
isers. Whereas the Socialist government had to some
extent benefited from a sympathetic hearing among
most students' unions since they were themselves
basically left-wing, it suffered because of the
ideological rift between it and those departments
which were the worst affected. Perhaps the government could have resisted the usual pressure exerted
upon it by students in France - demonstrations,
strikes and small-scale riots - but the students
were eventually joined by university staff and
hospital doctors of all ranks. This turned into the
longest medical strike in French history. Soon the
Prime Minister Pierre Mauroy intervened and set up a
study group to look at the question of the medical

schools. The result was that they were treated as a special case and granted greater independence than any other university department, including the right to continue specialised first-cycle studies.

However by the spring of 1983 opposition to the bill had spread to other departments, triggered by the word selection. Savary proposed what appeared to many students to be an alarming break with the past. He wanted entry to the second cycle of some higher education studies to be dependent not upon successful completion of the first cycle but upon the selection of the most suitable candidates by means, for example, of a competitive examination. The students were demonstrating not so much against selection since the continuation of the selection in the non-university sector raised no protest but against what was seen as their worsening chances of continuing their studies into the second cycle.

The students' fears for their own education were unfounded. Claude Jeantet's reaction to the student demonstrations was forthright: 'It's enough to listen to what the students are saying as individuals (...), when you question them it's obvious that they haven't seen, haven't read, haven't studied, haven't understood the text of the law'.(31) He was perfectly right especially since few seemed to realise that the new law was to affect only those entering the university for the first time in the autumn of 1984.

Nevertheless selection has always been a sensitive issue in the university sector even if it was accepted readily enough in other areas of the higher education system. The student revolt of 1968 had had its origins in a strike called in November 1967 by the students at Nanterre against the introduction the following year of a selection procedure in humanities and science courses for those who wanted to enter second-cycle studies. The better students would be allowed to pursue a 'long' course lasting two years and leading to research, the less good would take the 'short' course to a degree one year later. Serious trouble followed a similar attempt by Jean-Pierre Soisson when he tried the same sort of thing in 1976. Strikes lasting up to two months were a gauge of student displeasure.

The 1984 law was clearly a direct descendant of those earlier attempts to match the universities' output to society's needs. The number of students accepted for certain second-cycle courses would depend upon their likely job prospects. The debate on the law in 1983 in the National Assembly was

accompanied by large demonstrations, especially in
Paris. It was ironical that a bill inspired by the
principles of the 1968 law and which was being
debated fifteen years to the month after the famous
May events should now attract student action reminiscent of those earlier times. However, whereas the
1968 demonstrations led to the law, in 1983 it was
the law which led to the demonstrations. Another
difference was that the latest bill was far from
unopposed. In contrast to 1968, the opposition
voted solidly against it, citing such reasons as
the bill's emphasis on selection and over-representation of students on governing councils.

The selection issue was in fact something of a
red herring in that it was very restricted in its
consequences. There was never any question of it
affecting a majority of students. Selection already
existed for a small proportion of second-cycle
courses; only about 15,000 out of 260,000 had to pass
some sort of test in order to gain a place on certain
specialised degrees. Moreover there was no prospect
of this number being suddenly increased. Indeed
any growth would be small.(32) Those courses that
had traditionally depended on success in the first
part of the university studies would continue as
before. Thus virtually all the familiar degree
courses with no particular professional bias such as
modern languages, mathematics or history would
accept students without any further process of
selection. Savary had recognised that without a
massive injection of funds any change in the university system was bound to be gradual. It seemed more
likely that the professionalisation of courses
would only slowly change their character and as they
became more orientated towards the world of work and
accepted as a valid qualification, so they would
become popular with students and that only then
would a selection process be introduced. Put like
this, the professionalisation and selection process
smacked of a long-term commitment and moreover
needed staff from outside the universities - at the
very least in the short term - to angle courses
vocationally. Just how successful all this will be
in terms of finding students jobs can be judged from
1986 on when those entering the Savary-inspired
courses will have completed their first cycle. But
clearly it will be some years after that before any
proper measure can be made - and that is assuming
that universities do change in the way the 1984 law
foresaw. (Those departments introducing the new-
style courses changed their name from UER to UFR:

133

Unité de formation et recherche).

It is as well to mention at this point that post-graduate third-cycle studies were radically transformed by the 1984 law. In an effort to align post-graduate research degrees with those in other parts of Europe and America a new doctorate was instituted. The type that had for long dominated the university system had been the state doctorate or doctorat d'Etat which was an extensive piece of research which often took many years to complete. The (inevitably) less prestigious one was the third-cycle doctorate (doctorat du troisième cycle) which also involved the writing of a substantial thesis but which was usually completed in less time. The 1984 law effectively replaced both these by a single two-level doctorate. The first lasts between three and five years and is aimed to correspond to the British and American PhD. The second is a new departure since it can be awarded by universities to someone in recognition of their total output (for example, thesis, publications, technological advances and will be recognised as qualifying that person to direct research in a university.

The casualty in all this that has proved most shocking to the French university establishment is the doctorat d'Etat. The early proposals for the 1984 law simply mentioned a single doctorate and this raised for such senior academics as Maurice Duverger the spectre of a single university corps being created. (He need not have worried. A dual corps was retained.) Duverger claimed that the very survival of the university system depended in turn upon the survival of the doctorat d'Etat.(33) Perhaps the two-level doctorate will calm such fears and still provide the apparently necessary means of officially dividing the sheep from the goats.

University Administration

The law brought about more immediate major changes by re-structuring the governing body of the university. The previous single council was split into three: the Conseil d'administration, the Conseil scientifique and the Conseil des études et de la vie universitaire. The first has the responsibility for the general running of the university and it is this body which needs to approve policies adopted by the other two committees; the second is concerned with the conduct of the teaching and research; the

third has a fairly wide brief covering both the
organisation of courses as a whole and non-academic
student life. By allocating responsibility in this
tripartite manner, it was hoped that more detailed
attention could be paid to the full range of what
goes on in a university. But just as important, the
new councils were seen as a boost for the moribund
principle of participation so ardently desired in
1968. Student representation was improved and non-
university members were to be elected to all the
councils, the latter in an attempt to encourage
universities to be more outward-looking.

These proposals, unexceptional in appearance,
were to provoke some of the bitterest criticisms of
the bill, especially from the Right. The major one
was not so much at the level of general principles
but at that of detailed implementation. One part of
the proposals in particular aroused right-wing ire.
This was that university staff could not stand for
election to the council as individuals but in lists
of candidates and, although this once again seems
innocuous, it was a method of election which favoured the better-organised groups of staff. In practice
this meant those below the rank of professor. Fears
were aroused that those at the top of the university
hierarchy would be under-represented. But the
implications were regarded as serious not only
because those with the highest qualifications and
most responsibility might well be swamped but because
non-professional university staff tend (if they do
belong to one at all) to belong to trade unions with
a left-wing bias. The Right became alarmed at what
appeared to be nothing less than a plot by the Left
to ensure a tight grip on university administration.
In a debate on the Savary bill Raymond Barre accused
the government of giving trade unions (and therefore
politics) a role in French universities which they
should not have if the latter were to be autonomous
bodies.(34) One Parisian professor of law remarked
with deliberate irony that union representatives
'will be so numerous (...) that I am worried whether
the left-wing unions will be able to cope with the
demand'.(35) Pressure on the government became
sufficiently strong for the professors' representation to be increased, though only time will tell if
the fears of the Right were real.

Article 18 of the 1984 law states that higher
education institutions enjoy 'autonomie pédagogique
et scientifique, administrative et financière' and
great play is always made by the Ministry that
French universities are indeed autonomous. The

extent to which any institution can be so in any
country when it depends more or less completely upon
government money depends to a large extent upon the
political will of the government in power. French
universities have - like those in other countries -
found it difficult to resist determined government
pressure. As we have seen, Saunier-Séité during her
period at the Ministry of Education certainly made
life uncomfortable for universities when she chose.
The Socialist government continued with such traditional means of control as the system of supplementary grants to universities which finance those
courses that cannot be covered by the normal allocation. Many courses are taught by members of staff
not enjoying permanent tenure and universities
frequently have to go cap in hand to the Ministry to
ask for extra money. If it is not forthcoming,
courses close and the Socialist government, just like
its predecessors, has been forced to say no occasionally because of a policy of financial stringency.
In February 1983, for example, students went on
strike - ironically - in order to have lectures.
Just as potent as the withholding of grants is the
ability to favour those universities which develop
in ways approved of by the government. The Socialist
government allocated money to those prepared to
expand their electronics and computer science
departments, for example.
     There is perhaps little surprising about all
this since many universities in democracies experience these periods of what may be termed Voltarian
encouragement by governments and the degree of
auonomy enjoyed by a university is a matter sometimes
of subtle definition. Parts of the 1984 law however
illustrate just how firmly the margin for autonomous
action is drawn for French universities. For
example, Article 66 states: 'Institutions must adapt
their internal structure to the functions devolved
to them and in particular to the education that they
will be authorised to organise - according to the
objectives defined by the present law'. It is clear
that any freedom enjoyed by the universities is meant
to be exercised within limits that are carefully laid
down by the state. Yet Savary constantly urged
universities to diversify their courses and to use
their initiative, and to be fair to the Socialist
government it did support local initiatives in
universities when some wished to create new courses.
(36) The tight limits drawn by the state and
diversification within universities are not incom-
patible but the balance of these elements leads to

a certain type of autonomy, one that is further circumscribed by the French system of nationally validated degrees.

Degree validation

Although individual universities can award their own diplomas, all the important qualifications are validated by the state which is seen as the guarantor of their quality. The discussions aroused by the 1984 law once again raised the question as to whether or not this state involvement was beneficial. The principal argument against such close state interest in the award of first and higher degrees is that it stifles initiative, the very thing that Savary (and previous Ministers) have called for from the universities. This happens because the state (in other words the Ministry of Education) tries to ensure a certain uniformity in the courses, teaching methods and examinations in order to ensure that all degrees are of equal value. It is evident that the Ministry holds the whip hand in any dispute between itself and an individual university. We have seen for example how Saunier-Séité simply closed down virtually overnight large numbers of courses by claiming that they were not up to standard and this raises the query about just how accurately and fairly Ministry officials can monitor the huge diversity of university courses. The 1984 law set up a National Evaluation Committee (Comité national d'évaluation) which has the task of jointly evaluating with the universities (theoretically at least) their whole range of work and of 'recommending appropriate measures to improve the working of the institutions as well as the efficiency of the teaching and research'.

It has been argued that the time has come to scrap the system of nationally validated degrees and to allow individual universities to do their own validation, thereby creating better conditions for diversification. It is not an argument that touched Savary and it was not reflected in the 1984 law. This was because it was thought that the result would be competition between universities and an inevitable consequence of this would be the devaluation of the degree. Some universities would become less popular and so their awards would be regarded as second best. In other words, open competition for university places would be a disservice to students. This is not entirely fanciful given the dominance of Paris in the university system. It

137

attracts a quarter of all French university students
and has always possessed the most comprehensive
range of study facilities. One of the major complaints of the students in 1968 was of absentee
professors in the provinces who arranged to give all
their lectures on one day of the week and then
caught the train to Paris and spent most of their
time there. The situation seems hardly to have
changed in the intervening years since the Ministry
has frequently to put out circulars reminding
university staff of their residence obligations.
Paris remains a magnet and, if its influence has
been weakened somewhat over the years in various
spheres, it is still pre-eminent.

Nationally validated degrees therefore look like
remaining a feature of the university system at
least for the foreseeable future with all that this
implies in the way of Ministry of Education oversight of the courses. This could of course be a
merely nominal interest but in reality Ministers
have not been afraid to intervene, as we have seen.
But the universities' autonomy is compromised in
various other ways as well.

They have no control over the appointment of
staff since the number of posts are allocated on a
national basis and appointments are made by the
Ministry. Just how weak the position of the universities is in this matter is well illustrated by a
law(37) which forbids the university to transfer a
post from one establishment to another but which can
be done by the Ministry if the holder desires, even
against the wishes of that university. It is also
worthwhile repeating at this point that universities
have traditionally had little control over their
student intake and that any such control that has
surreptitiously grown up over the years has been
laid low by the 1984 act.

The close link between the state and the
higher education system is well illustrated by the
case of the CNRS (Centre national de la recherche
scientifique). This body, through some 45 specialist committees, oversees the bulk of academic
research in France. With an annual budget of nearly
eight billion francs supplied by the government, it
employs some 10,000 researchers and 15,000 technical
and administrative staff. But although many of
these are to be found on premises owned by the CNRS,
many are also employed in the universities and the
latter therefore depend heavily upon this central
organisation for their research funds. The CNRS
comes under the aegis of a government department –

that of Research - and both the president and direct-
or general are nominated by the Cabinet.
     The fact that national research is so intimate-
ly tied up with the vital interests of the state
and that a government department is so closely
involved in helping to run an almost monolithic
organisation makes it hardly surprising that the
CNRS has experienced political intervention in its
affairs. One of the first actions of Jean-Pierre
Chevènement when he was made Minister of Research in
the new socialist government in 1981 was to change
the method of electing members to the CNRS national
committee and to its specialist committees. The new
method enhanced the influence of those sections of
voters able to organise themselves in lists. The
suspicion (paralleling that evoked for the election
of candidates to university councils) was that this
strengthened the hand of the Left and trade unions,
and certainly trade unions were to benefit from one
or two new measures adopted by the new Minister.(38)
Chevènement was also keen to link the work done by
the CNRS with industry. Less emphasis was put on
research for its own sake and more upon the practical applications. Such a move did not receive full-
blooded support from all sections of the CNRS. Such
a reaction was perhaps not surprising but neither was
the fact that the Ministry who paid the piper wanted
to call the tune. It seems largely accepted that
matters of general policy fall within the purview of
the government of the day but where intervention
ends and interference begins is open to interpretation. When at the end of October 1981 Chevènement
suddenly replaced the director of social sciences
Christian Morrisson by Maurice Godelier, there was
a good deal of unfavourable reaction by the scientific community partly because it was thought that the
Minister had acted high-handedly and partly because
Godelier was appointed for his left-wing sympathies.

     Autonomy, then, is a relative term but in the
case of the French universities it has to be applied
in a restricted sense. Basically, the Ministry of
Education plays a large part in determining the
structure, courses and awards of the university.
Rather like the teacher training departments and
institutions in Britain in recent years, the French
universities are the minor partners of the government and are obliged to do what they are told. Yet
the presence of the government in the university is
still regarded as a guarantee of democracy and

equality, and it is this which allows the state the preponderant role in its relationship with the universities. Unfortunately, power corrupts and governments have often felt justified in acting arbitrarily whilst claiming to be acting for the good of all. Paternalism does not enhance communication and this explains why French universities are so jumpy. Ministers of Education are frequently surprised at the violence of university reaction but this comes in part from a fear by students and staff that their fate is not to any significant extent in their own hands and that the only way a government will take notice is if they take to the streets. Just how far greater representation on university councils will allay such fears remains to be seen but it is doubtful whether the basic pattern will alter as long as the government is clearly the guiding hand in all major decisions. But the basic pattern also depends to some extent upon the universities' willingness to play second fiddle. Students and staff complain long, loud and frequently when the Ministry of Education decision displeases them but the automatic recourse to demonstration and strike are always aimed at ministerial tinkering, rarely in support of real autonomy. Indeed the use of these well-worn university weapons in support of such a cause is almost inconceivable since both parties believe that it would be against their own best interests. An autonomous university is viewed as a threat since, freed of Ministry supervision, the university could do with students and staff as it liked. At least the state stands as guarantor of an individual's freedom. Liberty and equality flow from the Ministry of Education (fraternity is for tomorrow). Or at least so the reasoning runs.

NOTES

1.   Sections de techniciens supérieurs.
2.   The various sections, like some of the grandes écoles to which they lead, have built up their own slang. Thus the scientific classes are known as taupes, the literary ones as khâgnes and the business-orientated ones as prépas HEC (Hautes écoles commerciales).
3.   Ministère de l'Education Nationale, ONISEP, Guide pratique de la scolarité, 1982, p.39.
4.   Ministère de l'Education Nationale, Répères, p.167.
5.   Commission des titres d'ingénieurs, Liste

des écoles d'ingénieurs. (May 1983)

6.   I have followed Bruno Magliulo, Les Grandes écoles for both this group and the final (miscellaneous) one.

7.   Ministère de l'Education nationale, Répères, p.167.

8.   See, for example, Le Nouvel Observateur, 21.1.83.

9.   Also called ESC and, more familiarly, Sup.de Co.

10.   The Institut administratif des entreprises and the Institut d'études commerciales.

11.   Catherine Mackenzie makes an interesting comparison between ENA and the Civil Service College in her article 'The Ecole Nationale d'Administration and the Civil Service College', Comparative Education, March 1979.

12.   See J-L Crémieux-Brilhac, L'Education Nationale, p.158 et seq.

13.   L'Etat enseignant, p.276.

14.   Ministère de l'Education nationale, Répères, p.167.   In 1982-3 13.4% of the higher education pop-ulation was composed of foreign students.

15.   Décrets du 22 juin, 1966.

16.   For example, Raymond Aron, 'La crise dans l'université,' Le Figaro 2 avril, 1964.

17.   Society, Schools and Progress in France, p.148.

18.   Halls thought a Ministry of Education official was being flippant when he suggested this as one reason for some students registering. Op. cit. p.146.

19.   A.Prost, L'Enseignement en France, p.455.

20.   Nevertheless complaints were often heard that not enough was being done.   W.R.Fraser quotes the Dean of the Faculty of Science in Paris who declared that six years after he had been urgently asked for his development plans, the Ministry of Education had not even completed buying the necess-ary land.   Reforms and Restraints in Modern French Education, p.83.

21.   L'Administration de l'éducation: essai de bibliographie by M.Delclaux and J.Minot lists over 70 works on the May events published between 1968 and 1973 alone.

22.   A law of 12 July 1971 strengthened the Ministry's hand in this matter.

23.   Paul Milliez, Le Monde, 2 jan. 1974.

24.   Le Monde, 4.6.76.

25.   Conseil national de l'enseignement supér-ieur et de la recherche, a body created in the after-

math of the 1968 events.

26. _Journal de Dimanche_, 27.7.80.
27. _Syndicat national de l'enseignement supér-ieur_.
28. _Le Nouvel Observateur_, 6 mai 1983.
29. 'Exposé des motifs' _Cahiers de l'Education nationale_, mai 1983.
30. _Cahiers de l'Education nationale_, oct.1983.
31. _Le Nouvel Observateur_, 6.5.83.
32. Alain Savary confirmed this in the debate in the National Assembly on 24 May, 1983.
33. _Le Monde_, 21.5.83.
34. 'vous syndicalisez et vous politisez l'université', _Le Monde_, 26.5.83.
35. Jean-Michel de Forges in _L'Express_, 29.4.83.
36. 1984 also saw the creation of another state qualification, the DEUST (_diplôme d'études universitaires scientifiques et techniques_). This two-year course aims to train students in specific specialisms for which there is a demand. Thus at Aix-Marseille the DEUST prepares students for posts of responsibility in local government, Paris-XI in biotechnology, Clermont-Ferrand in the rehabilit-ation of the handicapped. See _Le Monde de l'Educ-ation_, nov.1984.
37. Loi du 17 juillet 1978.
38. For example the CNRS would henceforth rent premises for trade unions if it were unable to provide adequate accommodation. See 'CNRS: l'Etat savant', _L'Express_, 21.9.84. I have drawn freely on this article in this paragraph.

Chapter 5

HIGHER EDUCATION (2)   TEACHERS AND THEIR TRAINING

The training of teachers during the Fifth Republic
has been carried out in two institutions: the Ecole
Normale and the Centre pédagogique régional. This
fairly simple division however disguises a more
complicated classification applied to the types of
teachers working in schools. Apart from the various
categories of those who are in full-time temporary
posts there are four sorts of full-time permanent
teachers, each with different qualifications and
working conditions. These are the primary school
teacher and the three types of secondary-school
teacher: the PEGC (Professeur d'enseignement général
de collège), the professeur certifié and the professeur agrégé. The primary school teacher and the
PEGC are trained in the Ecole Normale and the other
two at the CPR. All are civil servants.
    Before looking in detail at the sort of train-
ing each type of teacher receives, it had better be
said that many French teachers are untrained. At
various times during the Fifth Republic demand out-
stripped supply. The consequence was that training
programmes were curtailed or simply ignored as
recruits were put directly into the classroom. The
raising of the school leaving age in the sixties
meant there was a shortfall of teachers and students
with degrees and primary school teachers were
drafted into the CES. Following the 1977 reform
creating the collèges, many teachers without initial
training were given PEGC status. Christian Beullac,
(the Giscardian Minister of Education from 1978 to
1981), fully intended that starting in 1980 no
primary school teachers would be recruited unless
they had been trained. But the best-laid plans of
mice and men... In 1981 the Socialist government
increased spending on education considerably in order
to keep teaching posts which the previous government

had intended axing. The result was that students had to begin their training as <u>instituteurs</u> and PEGC by taking classes full-time in schools. In other words, it has not been unusual for the French government to put the cart before the horse by first recruiting personnel and then later seeing to their training. Louis Legrand goes so far as to say that the practice has become so common that it is now institutionalised.(1) Union pressure has ensured that teachers without a teaching qualification are awarded one after completing a number of years' service.

Before 1969 those wishing to become primary school teachers went directly to an <u>Ecole Normale</u> at the end of the <u>troisième</u> and continued their education there. Only the final year of their course involved actual teacher training. After that date the minimum entrance requirement became the <u>baccalauréat</u>. This meant that those wishing to become primary school teachers had to complete their education at the <u>lycée</u> before embarking upon a two-year training programme.

The teaching profession has been associated for generations in the minds of Frenchmen with the idea of social promotion. The way for the son or daughter of a member of the humblest classes to leave the bottom rung of society was to become a teacher and the most accessible part of the profession was the position of <u>instituteur</u>. This idea of gradual ascension could still be typified by such successes as the former President of France, Georges Pompidou. His father had been a primary school teacher and his grandfather an agricultural worker. No wonder then that a good proportion of primary school teachers were often recruited from the lowest socio-economic classes. Although such an idea dies hard, it no longer corresponds to reality. The Fifth Republic has seen a radical change in the source of recruitment of primary school teachers. At the outset of the period nearly one-quarter were children of industrial workers but by the early 1980s this proportion had dropped to less than ten per cent. Only about five per cent were children of agricultural workers. It is the middle classes nowadays which provide primary schools with their teachers and three-quarters of these are women. Moreover, as Ida Berger has pointed out(2), such women are increasingly tending to marry into ever-higher socio-economic groups. It is not rare therefore that a primary school teacher's salary is not essential to her family and this fact, plus the reputation of women for being less openly critical, is said to have contributed towards the lessening of militancy in this sector.

It is interesting for a moment to look at the percentage of women teachers in the nursery and primary sectors. They form 98 per cent of the teachers in the former sector (99 per cent of the Heads) and 73 per cent in the latter (53 per cent of the Heads). Rightly or wrongly any profession that contains a high percentage of women tends to lose status and that of primary school teacher is in just that position. This is of course paralleled in many other countries. Teacher trade unions have long recognised this fact of life and therefore support positive discrimination in favour of male candidates seeking entry to training institutions. Since this militates against women on no other grounds than that they are women it was hardly surprising when there were occasional calls for the abolition of this form of discrimination as there were in 1975 by the Secretary of State for Women. However Christian Beullac yielded instead to pressure from the SNI to maintain the status quo and men continued to be awarded a disproportionate number of places for training.

Nevertheless the primary sector remains the most highly unionised one and its most important union by far is the SNI.(3) This has 70 per cent of primary school teachers as members and has thus always been a force to be reckoned with. It is the most powerful union in the teaching unions' umbrella organisation, the FEN(4), supplying for example, the majority of the latter's general secretaries over the years. It is also well represented on the consultative and joint committees at the various levels of educational administration - of which more will·be said in the final chapter. It was largely thanks to the efforts of the SNI that certain major improvements have been brought about in the sector. Some examples are the reduction of the working week from 30 to 27 hours in 1969, the granting of the equivalent of one year's in-service training during a (primary) teacher's career and the fixing of various maximum class sizes. The change in the training of teachers in 1979 was largely the outcome of negotiations between the SNI and the Ministry of Education. In addition it had long been pressing for the raising of primary school salaries in relation to those of other categories of teachers and it finally succeeded - because of its broadly left-wing sympathies - under President Mitterrand.

The SNI is also well known for having been the
originator of a network of insurance, banking and
retail organisations which it has built up for its
members. Teachers may belong to the CASDEN-BP(5)
for their banking, the MAIF(6) for insurance, the
MGEN(7) for medical insurance and CAMIF(8) - the
third biggest such organisation in France - for mail
order articles.

Despite such attractions, primary school teaching has gradually declined in prestige. Ironically
the effort to give all pupils better opportunities
by the generalisation of secondary studies with
the creation of the CES in the sixties exacerbated
the position of the primary school teacher in society. From that time on the teachers no longer
dispensed the only education that most pupils would
receive; they merely prepared them for a later
stage which by implication was more important.
Moreover the reforming zeal of teachers waned as
numerous studies especially during the last quarter
of a century or so indicated that the primary school
was not able to offer equality of opportunity to all
children regardless of social origin. The failures
in the system stubbornly remained disproportionately
of the lowest social classes and the successes
came disproportionately from the highest.(9) One of
the earliest dreams of the state education service
which persisted well beyond its true foundation at
the end of the last century was that society's
inequalities could be abolished by the sustained
efforts of primary school teachers. Despite its
rather utopian ring, such an idea had produced men
and women who regarded teaching as a vocation. The
father of the author Marcel Pagnol was such a man
and the latter brings alive the dedication of the
teaching profession in his autobiographical La Gloire
de mon père. But times change and harsh reality -
and sociological studies - have helped make teaching
today just another job.(10) It would be foolish
however to depict teachers of the eighties as less
worthy than those of former times. There never was
a golden age. It is too easily forgotten that
circumstances can change for the better. Who would
wish to bring back times that were often harsh for
both pupils and teachers? And who would wish
teachers to reinstate the rote learning of a restricted curriculum and the attempt to inculcate moral
precepts by pinning them to the wall?(11)

In recent years primary school teaching has
become somewhat more popular with men. This is
because in all probability it does offer stable

employment still in a world in which high unemployment has become familiar. Few of these however combine with their full-time duties the traditional spare-time role of the primary school teacher as assistant to the local mayor. This again was a throwback to the last century when the representatives of the state, particularly in rural France (and France remained largely so well into the twentieth century), the mayor and the local primary school teacher combined forces in an effort to establish both the Republic as France's proper form of government and secular education as superior to that dispensed by the local arch-rival, the priest and the Catholic school. Even before the coming of the Fifth Republic this form of school-local authority liaison was declining in popularity, though even today some 7,000 teachers still spend their Wednesdays (and often their weekends) involved in helping to run the local <u>commune</u>.

Each <u>département</u> in France has an <u>Ecole Normale</u> and it has been continuous government policy to offer higher education in all parts of the country, even in those areas with low populations. Competition to get into an <u>Ecole Normale</u> is keen with many more applications than places. There are two great attractions for any candidate to secure a place. Firstly each is guaranteed a job in a primary school if he completes his training and this is possible because the government sets targets for the number of teachers which will be needed and ensures that the <u>Ecoles Normales</u> admit only that number. It is a convenient way for the government to control the pupil-teacher ratio. The second attraction for the student is that, as a state employee, he is paid a wage immediately upon entering the <u>Ecole Normale</u>. The competition engendered by these advantages means that it is more difficult to gain entrance to an <u>Ecole Normale</u> than to a university, precisely because the university student does not enjoy either of these advantages.

In order to train as a primary (or nursery) school teacher candidates have had to sit a competitive examination at the <u>Ecole Normale</u> of their choice, (though it has not been unusual for someone to try two different examinations since the <u>Ecoles</u> do not all do their examinations at the same <u>time</u>). Basically, these are a fairly thorough test of a candidate's mental and physical suitability for the job as a nursery or primary school teacher. Two categories of candidates sit the competitive examination. The first is the school-leaver who has

passed his <u>baccalauréat</u> and the second is the primary school teacher without a permanent post. In
fact, union pressure usually helps the latter to
obtain a disproportionate number of places, though
to some extent the balance is restored in that those
in the first category who just fail often obtain a
temporary teaching post and are thus allowed into
the second category and sit as teacher candidates
the following year. As has already been mentioned,
male candidates are also treated more kindly by the
system,for if the <u>Ecole Normale</u> is in a <u>département</u>
which has a high proportion of women teachers in
nursery and primary education, a disproportionate
number of men are often allowed to pass in an effort
to counteract the <u>fémininisation</u> of the profession.
    What, then, does a candidate have to do in the
examination? Although a small amount of leeway is
given to each <u>Ecole Normale</u> by allowing them to fix
the details of the examination, its form is laid
down by the Ministry of Education so that candidates
all over France sit the same tests.
    The competitive examination itself comprises
three parts, each of which has to be passed before a
candidate may sit the next. The first consists of
two written comprehension tests each lasting three
hours. The first is based upon a text of general
interest and accompanied by questions, and one of
these might be a summary or extrapolation. The
second is a text of a scientific nature (though
'scientific' is very widely interpreted) which
demands an ability to understand and explain material
presented in a variety of ways. A candidate might,
for example, be asked to explain information contained in statistical tables or graphs. Both sections
of the first examination are meant to test not a
candidate's knowledge of a subject but his ability
to use the material presented. Interestingly
enough, quite a high proportion of the marks (six
out of twenty) for these tests is allocated for
spelling, writing and presentation, a weighting
which indicates their relative importance. The
second part of the competitive examination is particular to the <u>Ecole Normale</u> since it largely concentrates upon a candidate's physical suitability. The
tests are divided into three. The first assesses
the candidate's aptitude for teaching physical
education and games. It had better be said that it
is mere competence that is sought and not a high
competitive standard. This involves throwing balls
at targets, walking an inclined beam, completing an
obstacle course, a simple exercise on parallel ropes

and continuous running (fifteen minutes for women, twenty minutes for men). Also tested is the ability to swim: diving in and swimming some fifty metres whilst negotiating various obstacles such as a submerged ring and retrieving an object from the bottom of the pool. These latter exercises are not too formidable for candidates since all French children are taught to swim before they leave primary school. In addition general competence and the ability to work with others in a team game is examined practically. Recent ministerial instructions - thoughtfully - do not oblige pregnant women to do all this. The second part requires a candidate to read aloud to ensure he has a suitable voice. He also has to recognise pitch, rhythm and tone in musical instruments. For the third part the candidate must produce a piece of art or craft work.

Most candidates know pretty well what to expect in the first two examinations and indeed most of them pass these. It is the third which really determines the ones who are to make up the Ministry of Education's quota for that département. This is an oral examination in which the candidate has forty-five minutes to prepare a general passage (teachers get something on education) and half an hour to persuade the examiners (probably including a member of the Inspectorate) that he is worthy of featuring among the small band of successful candidates who will train to be primary teachers.

Major changes in the training of primary school teachers were instituted in 1979 in the Ecoles Normales. The government was anxious to raise the standard of training and one obvious way that this could be achieved was to lengthen the course from two to three years. The range of subjects then being offered to pupils in the collèges made it imperative that the instituteur was better educated himself particularly since henceforth all pupils would be given the chance to sample the full range of the secondary-school curriculum. Correspondingly the Ecoles Normales were to place greater emphasis on the training they gave outside the three Rs. One other motive for change - and one that is frequently heard from successive governments - was a desire to lessen schools' tendency for introspection and to open them more to the outside world. Thus student teachers were to be offered courses which gave them the opportunity to reflect upon the nation's economy and politics. In addition came the evergreen demand that courses were henceforth to match more closely educational theory to practice. Virtually all aspects of the students' courses were to be applicable to the school situation.

The first term of the three-year course is spent largely sampling as wide a range of classes as possible, from the nursery school to the first year of the collège whilst the rest of the year is spent following a foundation course common to all Ecoles Normales. It is only at the end of the first year that students are asked to sign an undertaking to work for the state for seven years. Previously their signature was demanded before entering (binding for a period of ten years), a rather risky business since students had little idea how they would react to teaching. The first-year visits at least allow a more informed choice to be made. The benefit of such a change is not necessarily solely to the student's advantage for, if his progress is unsatisfactory during the first year, the Ecole Normale can more easily ask him to leave.

The 1979 reform also introduced the modular course to the Ecole Normale.(12) A student follows ten compulsory modules in his first year each assessable and which must be passed before entry into the second year. During the remaining two years another twenty modules are added making thirty in all. There are two basic types of module: those that are compulsory and those from among which a student is permitted a choice. Of course, Paris lays down those areas which it considers form a necessary grounding for the student and moreover they make up two-thirds of the whole course. They are: French (3 modules), mathematics (2), science, history, geography, music, art, craft (4), physical education (2), the nursery school (1), child development (2), general pedagogy (2) and the economic, social, cultural and institutional world (2). The second type of module is simply one which extends a student's knowledge in the areas already mentioned, and Ecoles Normales have greater freedom to organise this type as they see fit, perhaps responding to a locally felt need. The average student's timetable is a heavy one since he is supposed to do some 24 hours a week on this work plus six hours on individual study. In addition vacations are partly spoken for since not only is the Ecole Normale student obliged to spend part of them helping to supervise children's leisure activities (acting for example as an assistant in a centre de vacances) but also to experience the world of work by being attached to a business or commercial concern - the latter in an evident effort to widen his horizons.

It was hoped that the introduction of the mod-
ular-based course would bring more flexibility in
that a modicum of choice would be available to the
student and that it would enable the Ecole Normale
to organise the detail of its courses as it saw fit.
Moreover the new approach would make it that much
easier to monitor student progress with an average
of four modules to be passed per term.

An interesting innovation aimed at raising the
standard of the primary school teacher's studies and
once again at widening his horizons was the association of the universities in the training course.
Certain parts of it are now followed at the local
university and at the end of the three-year period
the students are awarded the university qualification, the DEUG. Since this is one of the student's
final awards, it is evident that France does not at
the moment view primary school teachers' studies as
of degree level.

One aspect of the Ecole Normale training worth
mentioning is the part played in it by the local
primary inspector. As we shall see in the final
chapter, the inspector is a key figure in the education service with responsibility, for example, for
organising in-service activities. As the superior
of all primary school teachers in his area, he is
ideally situated to help place students in schools.
Here then is a potentially fruitful liaison between
training institutes and the profession in practice.
In reality it is not always a relationship which
prospers. The inspector has often been jealous of
his authority and has been careful that it is not
challenged, and as gatekeeper for school access he is
in a powerful position. The Ecole Normale staff
therefore depend very much upon the good will of the
inspector who sees his first responsibility as being
to the Ministry of Education and the interpretation
of its circulars rather than to the Ecole Normale.
The relationship between the Ecole Normale tutor
and the inspector has therefore not necessarily been
a warm one. The tutor has overall responsibility
for the training of students but the inspector has a
role in assessing those students in school when they
are on teaching practice. Thus although it is the
tutor who belongs to the panel of examiners which
awards the final teacher's certificate, the CFEN
(Certificat de fin d'études normales), it is the
inspector who is involved in the award of the student's final practical certificate, the CAP (Certificat d'aptitude pédagogique) without which of course
the student will not be given a teaching post. In a

way therefore - and this is something Ecole Normale
staff are acutely aware of - the inspector has overseen the tutor's work. Of course, the poor student
may be caught between two masters if there is not
general agreement between them about teaching
methods.(13)
     Other criticisms have been voiced about the
primary teacher's training programme. One is that
the modular structure relies too much upon assessment with students furiously working to gain an
average four credits per term. To many students
there is too much stick and precious little carrot.
Moreover many modules seem to have fallen into the
trap endemic to this type of course structure: a
lack of coordination between the various self-contained units. Despite the aims of the new courses,
the criticism subsists that they do not relate
sufficiently to what happens in schools. One final
source of discontent directly associated with the
1979 reform is that the DEUG awarded to students is
deficient as a first step towards gaining a degree
by further part-time study. This is because the
options offered to Ecole Normale students have been
peculiar to them (often cutting them off from university students) and thus do not form an acceptable
foundation course to many of the options that are
available in second-cycle university studies.
     The other categories of teacher, trained specif-
ically to work in the secondary sector, are the
agrégé, the certifié and the PEGC. Those working in
the LEP have the same contracts as the other types.
The numbers of teachers with each type of qualification working in full and part-time permanent posts
in 1982-3 are as follows: Agrégés (20,385), Certifiés
(89,167), PEGC (73,419), LEP teachers (44,790).
Some 35,000 teachers work in the secondary sector
without a permanent post.
     The PEGC teachers are trained in Centres de
PEGC which were created in 1960.(14) Each centre is
attached to that Ecole Normale which is situated in
the chief town of the académie and each comes under
the authority of the director of the Ecole Normale.
The course lasts three years though there is provision for direct entry into the second year. To
qualify for the shortened course candidates must
have a university first-cycle diploma in which one
or more of the following subjects feature: mathematics, physics, chemistry,biology, geology, classics,
French, a modern language, history and geography.
In other words, a candidate's subject must correspond
to one taught in secondary schools.

Entry to a centre is not automatic for, like all teacher training courses in France, admission to them (and their successful completion) guarantees a job and thus competition is again keen. For direct entry into the second year for instance, although a first-cycle diploma is required, it is often the minimum qualification needed. The examination set by the centre for entry is a competitive one with the number of places offered going to those with the highest marks. Candidates sitting the examination might well have a first or higher degree - the guarantee of a job attracting university students of course. In such circumstances it is often the primary school teacher with relatively few paper qualifications who finds entry difficult. The Ministry of Education occasionally has to remind centres that they should be looking more sympathetically at such cases.(15)

The major difference between a PEGC and other categories of secondary school teacher is that he is trained to teach two subjects, though, as the name implies, a PEGC teaches only in a collège and not a lycée. But if he is expected to teach two subjects he is not free to train for any combination. The Ministry of Education has laid down(16) the exact pairings and the centres are correspondingly divided into the appropriate teaching sections. These are:

Section I	-	Arts(17) plus history and geography
Section II	-	Arts plus a foreign language
Section III	-	Mathematics plus physics and technology
Section IV	-	Natural sciences plus physics and technology
Section V	-	French plus Latin
Section VI	-	Arts plus physical education and games
Section VII	-	Mathematics plus physical education and games
Section VIII	-	Natural science plus physical education and games
Section IX	-	Arts plus music
Section X	-	Mathematics plus music
Section XI	-	Arts plus art and craft
Section XII	-	Mathematics plus art and craft
section XIII	-	Handicrafts

There are no trained PEGC officially offering combinations that cross these section boundaries; for instance, history and biology or a foreign language and mathematics. This is not to say however that the exigencies of individual school timetables do not sometimes oblige PEGC (and indeed other categories of staff) to teach a wider range.

The three-year course is not the sole responsibility of the centre but has from the very beginning involved the local university. Indeed virtually the whole of the first year is spent there. It is only in the second year that students begin to spend most of their time in the centre. Again the timetable is heavy with up to 25 hours per week devoted to lectures. These first two years are in addition exclusively concerned with raising the student's level of competence in his academic subjects and the first part of the final qualification the CAPEGC(18) is appropriately called theoretical since it has nothing to do with teaching. It is in the third year that students learn to teach and go out into schools on teaching practice. It is the student's performance in schools which determines whether or not he passes the practical part of his teaching certificate. Once again the inspectorate is involved in the assessment, indeed for the practical part of the examination the student will have at least two people watching him at the back of the class: the inspector and his tutor. But he might also have the headmaster and that particular class's normal teacher.

The remaining two categories of secondary school teacher hold permanent posts by virtue of the fact that they possess either the CAPES(19) or the agrégation(20). Both training programmes are basically the same though there are important differences of detail. To some extent the programmes are similar in structure to that of the PEGC in that there are two parts: one theoretical and the other practical. The break between those parts is however more complete. The most difficult section of the programmes is the first, theoretical one. Yet the theory which the candidates must know has nothing to do with teaching. It is simply an extension of their degree studies. The range of subjects available is a wide one, much wider in the case of the agrégation in particular than that offered to the PEGC candidate. The CAPES has about a dozen options, the agrégation over twenty, including among others philosophy, Slav languages, physics, economics, engineering of various sorts, social sciences and physical education (a recent addition). The first part of both the CAPES and the agrégation is a competitive examination. Only by

being one of the few to pass this can a candidate
gain access to studies in how to teach. A closer
look at the structure of the part-one examinations
will illustrate what the student is up against. We
shall take as our example the examinations in a
foreign language: English.

In addition to its basic theoretical and practical division, the examination is further sub-divided.
The first part is composed of both a written and an
oral section. Once again, the first must be successfully negotiated before access is allowed to the
second. There are four papers in the written part
of both the CAPES and the agrégation and although
it is convenient to treat both together, there are
no papers common to both. The first consists of a
single question on a work of literature to be answered in English. It lasts four hours in the case of
the CAPES, seven in the case of the agrégation. In
1984 the former had on its syllabus Wordsworth and
Coleridge, The Lyrical Ballads, Orwell, 1984 and
Ellison, The Invisible Man, the latter had in addition: Shakespeare, Coriolanus and Gaskell, North-
South. Thus the agrégation candidate might have the
words 'Corruption in Bleak House' staring up at him
(or more probably her in a modern language examination) from the middle of the examination paper and
seven hours ahead to organise an answer(21). The
next two are translation papers, one into, the other
from, English; the CAPES allowing three hours, the
agrégation four. The examinations differ for the
fourth paper, with the CAPES candidate having to
analyse several paragraphs of a literary text over
four hours and the agrégation candidate having seven
hours to answer a question from one of three optional papers: the first on literature(22), the second
on British and American society(23), the third a
linguistic analysis of a literary text.

The oral examinations for the CAPES and agrégation differ. The CAPES has two parts each with two
hours preparation time and forty minutes before a
panel of examiners. The first examination is an
analysis of a short story and the second a comment-
ary on a non-literary subject, often an article
from a magazine or newspaper. The candidate speaks
in English and is marked upon his level of competence in the language.

In the agrégation, apart from two translation
examinations, there is one that is a nod in the
direction of the candidate's presumed future career;
this is the presentation of a so-called lesson. In
fact, this paper is about as far from a classroom

lesson as it is possible to be. The candidate is
given five hours to prepare a literary subject and
present it for thirty minutes to the panel. The
flavour of such presentations can to some extent be
savoured by a few examples of the type of question
asked: symmetries and contrasts in The Winter's
Tale, literalness in The Changeling, the family
metaphor(s) in John Bull, God in Blake's poetry(24).
The final paper is an analysis of a literary social
or linguistic nature based upon a given passage.

Two things emerge forcefully from the above
outline. First, the agrégation is the more difficult
of the two and the consequence of this is that it has
the greater prestige, plus more material advantages,
as we shall see later. Second, the aim of such
competitive examinations is to show that the men and
women who gain these qualifications possess a high
degree of competence in their subject. It is in any
case necessary for those wishing to sit the CAPES
to be in possession of a degree and those wishing to
sit for the agrégation to have a higher degree. But
the intended effect of the competitive examinations
is to ensure that only the best candidates enter
teaching. Of course it has to be remembered that
most candidates have been through the university
system, though the examinations are open to all,
including students of the grandes écoles. Nevertheless those in possession of the CAPES and especially
the agrégation are people with a thorough subject
knowledge. It may be objected that there remains a
heavy bias towards literature in the particular
example used but this objection can be countered by
saying that non-literary options play an important
part in both examinations and that no candidate without considerable competence in the spoken language
can hope to pass.

Courses preparing students for these theoretical
examinations are run at the Ecoles Normales Supérieures and many universities. For those unable to
get to such courses, there always exists the CNEC,
the national correspondance course centre under the
aegis of the Ministry of Education(25).

Both examinations have a reputation for being
very difficult to pass and this reputation has been
enhanced as the years have gone by because of the
growing number of candidates. Among students it is
widely believed that the chances of success are so
small that luck has as much to do with passing as
anything else. The examinations are certainly the
cause of a good deal of anxiety for although it is
possible to obtain a teaching post on the strength

of one's degree, that post is not a permanent one and has to be surrendered as soon as a qualified candidate appears on the scene. Moreover, without the CAPES or the agrégation, a teacher cannot be paid the full rate for the job, even if he is doing exactly the same work as a qualified teacher. It is little wonder then that many unqualified full-time teachers sit these examinations each year.

To give some idea of the pressure upon candidates, it is sufficient to look at the figures involved (in English again). In 1982 which, because of the arrival of the Socialist government, was a year with an unusually high number of posts on offer, there were 360 teaching jobs for those who passed the CAPES. There were 4,555 candidates. 120 posts were allocated for the agrégation. There were 1,693 candidates. It is these sorts of figures which are the despair of candidates and indeed many sit both examinations in one year in an effort to reduce the odds(26).

In fact however the odds are less formidable than the above figures suggest. A large proportion of the candidates, usually between one-quarter and one-third, do not turn up for the examination and many more are poorly prepared. In the CAPES written examination in English in 1982 the average mark out of twenty was between four and seven depending on the paper(27). Percentage success rates in the various disciplines have fluctuated over the years although the chances of success are of course affected by the number of posts the state chooses to allocate to different disciplines in different years. It has for example encouraged those with science qualifications. The following table shows the percentage success rates in the broad discipline areas in the agrégation and CAPES for 1983(28).

Table 5.1

Agrégation	%
Literary	26.3
Modern Languages	17.3
Scientific	50.7
Artistic	5.7

CAPES	%
Literary	34.6
Modern Languages	20.3
Scientific	38.1
Artistic	7.0

Suggestions for the reform of the system have been made for many years. Basically, these have called for the amalgamation of the two types of examination. It has also been proposed that the agrégation should be a dual preparation offering candidates the option to go in either for teaching or for research. Certainly the agrégation was always meant to carry with it the possibility of later research work and a good many agrégés in the past have gone into university teaching. Today things are different and few such posts are available, though the agreement to serve the state (for five years) does not oblige the agrégé to go into teaching; the French state has many doors. Nevertheless the agrégé does tend in the eighties to go into secondary teaching, gravitating towards the lycée.

That happy band of pilgrims who came at the head of the lists of the theoretical part of the CAPES and the agrégation assemble at a Centre pédagogique régional(CPR) for a year-long practical course which now concentrates upon preparing them to become teachers. Like the Ecole Normale, the CPR was in existence before the Fifth Republic(29). In contrast to the Ecole Normale and the Centre PEGC, the CPR usually has no permanent teaching staff. Its director is a regional inspector (see the final chapter) who has other responsibilities besides running the Centre. The director drafts in other inspectors and teachers to work part-time with him in putting together a viable course. From the very beginning students work four or five hours per week in a school and this continues to the end of the year. In addition they do two teaching practices thereby adding up to another six hours per week for eighteen to twenty weeks. They also spend six weeks in a business or commercial concern. While they teach in a school, a teacher whose class the student takes is designated as the student's counsellor (and is paid for it).

The training of technical education staff follows closely the pattern of training at the

different levels already outlined. Students intending to enter the technical lycées simply spend an
extended practice in an industrial concern. Those
entering the LEP go to an ENNA (Ecole normale
nationale d'apprentissage) for two years, after
having completed two or three years' higher education.
Those teaching general subjects in an LEP train in
two subjects like the PEGC.

When students finally qualify they are allocated
particular posts; they do not apply for them. They
are allowed to express preferences for areas and
these preferences may be taken into account - or
they may not. At least the primary school teacher
will be offered a post in the département in which
he trained (and in which he probably originated) and
the PEGC will be sent somewhere within the académie,
already quite a large area. But the certifié and
the agrégé, since their examinations are national
ones, may be posted anywhere in France. It is not
unusual for young teachers to be sent to the other
end of France from their home nor for husband and
wife who are both qualified to be separated by
hundreds of miles in their postings. Some young
teachers prefer to spend a substantial part of their
earnings on maintaining two flats and on travelling
so that they may spend their weekends in their home
town. Each year however the Ministry of Education
publishes lists indicating areas in which posts are
available and changes are frequent, though only a
minority of requests are satisifed. It is worth
mentioning that the most popular postings are those
in the southern half of France and - of course -
Paris.

There are, then, four categories of teachers
working in French schools and little is more likely
to provoke a reaction than to remind them of it for
this division brings marked differences in working
conditions and status. The primary school teacher
works 27 hours a week, the PEGC 21, the certifié 18
and the agrégé 15, in theory at least for in reality
the secondary school teachers are usually obliged to
work an additional two hours. Moreover the teachers'
rate of pay is in inverse proportion to the number
of hours worked. This is because, as civil servants,
they are based upon different points of the scale
applied to all government employees. Thus the
primary school teacher starts at the lowest position
of the four categories and can never reach the
highest point of the PEGC who is just above him on

the scale. And so on up. Such a system might arouse less controversy if these categories worked in different schools but, apart of course from the primary school teacher, they do not. The perfect example of this is to be found in the collège where all three categories of secondary school teacher will probably be taking the same sorts of classes and following the same syllabuses and yet being paid differently for it. For years past teachers have been urged by the Ministry of Education to work more cooperatively (as we have seen in previous chapters) but this basic inequality of treatment does little to help. The minority of agrégés point to their tougher training and so on down the line. In Pour un collège démocratique Louis Legrand recently suggested the obvious solution of giving all teachers the same number of teaching hours (he suggested sixteen) but it has been calculated that something in the order of 35,000 new posts would have to be created to cover the number of hours relinquished by teachers now in employment(30). Of course the cost would be enormous. Another solution might be to give all teachers more hours (say twenty) but the certifiés and the agrégés would probably see this as an attack on their status and working conditions and in any case would expect to be paid at the (higher) supplementary hour rate. This in turn would prove expensive. Just how much resistance this might provoke can perhaps be gauged by the very fact that Legrand chose not to suggest it. Certainly the Société des agrégés is ever watchful.

On top of his basic salary a teacher receives various allowances, most of them the more substantial the further up the hierarchy he is placed. Thus he receives an allowance for travel to school, examining, taking part in a conseil de classe and for helping a student on teaching practice. Apart from the two hours extra per week which a teacher is contractually obliged to fulfil if necessary (but for which he gets paid at a higher rate), he can often work extra hours if he wishes. Like all civil servants, teachers receive extra pay for any children they might have. Other allowances are paid for taking preparatory classes in lycées and primary school teachers are either given accommodation or paid an allowance in lieu.

Extra money may also come in because of an especially good mark awarded to him by the inspector- a system to which we shall return in the final chapter. Teachers may also attempt to go up a category either by sitting the competitive examinations already described or by putting their names forward to be promoted by virtue of their past teaching record, though usually only a ninth of the posts offered in each category every year are alloc- ated by this last method. However the Socialist government has speeded up this process and also the granting of permanent status to those on temporary contracts (without getting teaching qualifications). But promotion into the inspectorate or to such posts as headmaster or deputy head is also possible, though PEGC may not become headmasters of lycées. Teachers who move into such hierarchies are sent on courses before taking up their posts. A headmaster, for example, has an eleven-week course followed by various meetings thereafter. Upon becoming a head- master, a teacher expects to leave the classroom for ever.

As a footnote to this chapter, it should be said that major changes are on the way for the train- ing of teachers in France. The Peretti Report, commissioned by Alain Savary, proposed many alter- ations to the present system including a far greater emphasis on in-service training. It is impossible to say at the time of writing (January 1985) to what extent the many proposals in the report will be carried out but they include such innovations as the greater alignment of the various types of initial training for those entering secondary schools and the (theoretical) introduction of training courses for university teachers. Thus far the French govern- ment have only seized upon the sector that can be expected to offer least resistance (having been the most reformed part of the training system): the Ecoles Normales. In a speech made in Toulouse in November 1984 Jean-Pierre Chevènement gave the broad outline of future developments. The primary school teacher's training is to be extended to four years with greater university participation and the PEGC is to work for a degree-level qualification (with some possibility of his concentrating on a single subject in future). The other categories of second- ary school teacher trainees are to have the practical part of their course strengthened by increasing the time spent in schools.

NOTES

1. Pour une politique démocratique de

l'éducation, (PUF 1977)
    2.   Les instituteurs d'une génération à une autre.
    3.   Syndicat national des instituteurs. In fact this union includes an important section of secondary-school teachers, the professeurs d'enseignement général de collège which is why the union's full title is SNI-PEGC.
    4.   Fédération de l'Education nationale.
    5.   Caisse d'aide sociale de l'Education nationale - Banque populaire.
    6.   Mutuelle assurances des instituteurs de France.
    7.   Mutuelle générale de l'Education nationale.
    8.   Cooperative des adhérents de la mutuelle des instituteurs de France.
    9.   See, for example, Christian Baudelot and Roger Establet, L'Ecole primaire divise.
    10.   A survey revealing much discontent among teachers is to be found in Michel Jamet, 'Des instituteurs mal à l'aise' in Esprit, nov-déc 1982.
    11.   An amusing depiction of such futility is given (once again by Pagnol) in Topaze, (1928)
    12.   Circulaire du 26 juin, 1979.
    13.   See, for example, Gilles Laprévote, La Formation des instituteurs primaires.
    14.   Décret du 21 oct. 1960.
    15.   See, for example, the circulaire du 2 sept. 1969: 'It is appropriate not to lose sight of the fact that centres must first accept those primary-school teachers wishing to train to teach in the collèges and particularly those teachers working in a collège without the qualification necessary for a permanent post.'
    16.   Arrêté du 16 mars, 1970.
    17.   This usually means French or classics.
    18.   Certificat d'aptitude au professorat d'enseignement général de collège.
    19.   Certificat d'aptitude au professorat de l'enseignement secondaire. The CAPET is the equivalent qualification in technical education.
    20.   The holder of the first qualification is known either as a capétien or a (professeur) certifié. The holder of the second is known as a (professeur) agrégé.
    21.   This question was set in 1983.
    22.   The 1984 syllabus was Vaughan, Silex Scintillans, Sterne, Tristram Shandy, Eliot, Murder in the Cathedral, Poe, Poems, Nabokov, Ada.
    23.   In the same year the syllabus was: Hollywood 1929-69: mirror, symbols, communication;

The English in India during the Victorian period; the relationship of central and local government 1945-82.

24. These were a few of the subjects offered in 1983.

25. The Centre national d'enseignement par correspondance has six centres (Paris, Grenoble, Lille, Lyon, Rouen, Toulouse). These cover a huge range of courses from primary school to the agrégation for those who are only able to study at home. The tuition is free though there is a modest annual charge for registration. In 1982-3 this ranged from 200 to 405 francs depending upon the course.

26. This was a particularly successful tactic for nineteen candidates in 1982 who passed the English examinations in both.

27. Rapports de jurys de concours (1982) CAPES, Anglais.

28. Ministère de l'Education Nationale, Répères, p.93. In the same year 871 candidates passed the CAPET and 280 the CAPEPS.

29. Circulaire du 12 juin, 1952.

30. Jehanne Bolon, 'Quels maîtres pour quelles écoles?' Esprit, nov-déc. 1982.

Chapter 6

EDUCATIONAL ADMINISTRATION AND THE INSPECTORATE

The administration of the French education service
is centred on Paris and largely controlled from
there. Its most important element, from the point
of view of teachers, pupils and parents, is the
inspectorate. This three-tiered corps is involved
not simply in school inspections but in virtually
every aspect of the administration of the education
service. Although this chapter will deal with all
the most important elements within the administration, it will concentrate upon the role of the French
inspectorate.

Paris: the Ministry of Education
The organisation and history of the Ministry of
Education under the Fifth Republic is complicated
and can only be touched upon briefly in a work
which aims to cover the whole of the education
system. The exact composition and responsibilities
of the numerous services and committees centred upon
the rue de Grenelle would require a volume of its
own. We shall thus confine our examination to those
aspects we consider to be of most relevance to gaining an insight into the working of the system.
        The Minister of Education lost some of his
responsibilities under the presidency of Giscard
d'Estaing when the universities were placed under an
autonomous secretary of state and the administration
of the teaching of physical education and games was
hived off under a Ministry for the Quality of Life
which, as may be assumed from its title, held
rather a broad and disparate brief. The arrival of
the Left in power in 1981 however once again gave
the Minister overall responsibility for the whole of
the education system. The epithet nationale -
dropped by Giscard - was also restored to the title

164

<u>Ministre de l'Education</u>. There seems to have been little significance in either the disappearance or restoration. Some saw its disappearance as a sign that Giscard intended devolving significant powers to local areas but there was little subsequent support for such a suggestion. Perhaps he viewed the shortened title (the Ministry of Defence suffered the same foreshortening) as more in keeping with his image as a modern technocrat. He had after all a reputation for being closely interested in minutiae. The restoration of <u>nationale</u> in 1981 by the socialists may have simply been political tit-for-tat.

According to the French Constitution, the Minister of Education is appointed to his post by the President on the advice of the Prime Minister. This appears to give the Prime Minister the job of drawing up a list of suitable candidates which the President then appproves but in reality de Gaulle set his seal upon the office of President and it is the holder of this office who often chooses the ministers. In any case, if the person appointed is a <u>député</u>, he has to resign that office since the constitution does not allow any minister to hold both positions concurrently. The Minister of Education then sets about appointing his team of advisers or <u>cabinet</u>. This is an entirely personal choice and it is this <u>cabinet</u> with its ministers which takes the important executive decisions for the ministry. To become a member of such a <u>cabinet</u> often proves a fillip to the career of the appointee. However, since his appointment depends absolutely upon the Minister, he will probably fall when his Minister does. Nevertheless, since he is likely to be a member of France's administrative elite, he will soon be reintegrated into public or private administration. There is a tendancy for such ministerial advisory teams to be inbred as they are frequently the product of a system of promotion centred on Paris and thus often view problems from that perspective. Moreover the relative power of the <u>cabinet</u> tends to take decision-making out of the hands of the permanent officials of the Ministry who are thus more firmly tied to the role of implementing policy rather than participating in it. However, if the Minister can appoint whoever he wishes to his <u>cabinet</u>, since 1948 he can only appoint a maximum of ten members(1). Ultimately of course the Minister bears the responsibility for everything that happens within the Ministry and within the service as a whole. French public law does not allow the Minister to hand over his powers to anyone else though in

165

practice he cannot possibly receive all the information coming into the Ministry nor take all the
decisions and so delegation of responsibility is
inevitable.

The Minister of Education suffers in a way that
is perhaps unique to his Ministry (though not to
France). Everyone in the country has had personal
experience of the education system and thus often
has his or her own ideas on the way it should be
run. Not that the Minister has directly to contend
with the opinions of the whole population of France -
that privilege falls to the teachers - but he has
often to contend with a Prime Minister or President.
Michel Debré took over the responsibility of the
Ministry of Education for a short while at the end
of 1959 and the beginning of 1960 whilst still
remaining Prime Minister and gave his name to one of
the most important laws on private education. Georges
Pompidou, an ex-teacher, spoke in education debates
when Prime Minister and retained a keen interest in
the subject when President. Giscard too was a
prime mover in educational reform.

This generalised experience of the system may
be the reason why so many Ministers themselves have
been keen to leave their mark. Few have been those
who have been unwilling to undertake reform of part
or even sometimes of the whole of the education
service. Yet two basic factors (besides that of
vested interest of groups within the service) have
militated against any one Minister achieving concrete
change. One is time. Eighteen men have held the
post between 1958 and 1985(2) making the average
tenure eighteen months. Any reform of the education
system of necessity takes time to be implemented
(leaving aside the probability that it will not be
put into practice in the form first envisaged) and
so Ministers have tended to work on reforms whose
implementation they would never see during their
tenure of office. Indeed their day-to-day problems
have often been those involving the implementation
of reforms begun under a previous Minister.

The other major factor is the size of the
French education service. Since it is the state
which is the employer of all teaching staff and most
of the administrative and ancillary workers, the
Ministry of Education has on its books over one
million workers (some 600,000 of them teachers) plus
fourteen million pupils and students. In 1984 over
sixteen per cent of the state budget was spent on
education. It has been said the French education
system is the fourth largest organisation in the

world after the Chinese and Russian armies and
General Motors.(3)   Nevertheless there has always
existed a strong desire, evident in all sections of
the service, to maintain centralised control since
this is seen as a guarantee of impartiality against
local arbitrariness.   Thus it is the state which
monitors all examinations.   There might be regional
variations in the questions set for the <u>baccalauréat</u>,
for example, but the Ministry of Education, through
its Paris-based inspectorate, has oversight of these
variations by being involved in the setting and
marking of the papers.   If the day ever existed when
the Minister of Education knew when all the pupils of
a certain year group were studying a particular
subject, it has long since passed.   How could it be
otherwise?   The education service is far too large
and diversified for any single person to control it
in anything but the most imperfect way.

The CSEN

Of the various consultative committees operating at
the national level, the <u>Conseil supérieur de l'Education nationale</u> is the most important.   Like several
such organisations it has a long history but it will
suffice to say that before 1965 it was an inward-
looking body by virtue of the fact that no one who
was not employed by the Ministry of Education was a
member of it.   From 1965 on however seats were given
to people from other sectors who had an interest in
the good functioning of the education service, even
if they were not directly paid by it.   However, the
attempt to improve the council's function as a
sounding board has meant that it has grown in size.
It now has 84 members.   Apart from the Minister of
Education himself who chairs its meetings, the Council has representatives from the private sector,
educational administration (including inspectors),
parents' associations, various unions and teachers.
     The Council has two basic functions.   The first
is as a consultative committee when the Minister
wants opinions on educational questions of national
interest and the second is as an appeals committee
in cases of disciplinary action taken against
teachers.   The Minister must consult it and indeed
such consultation is enforced by law in certain
cases, and the Council expects to examine education
bills and various circulars emanating from the
Ministry.   However, since the committee is only a
consultative one, the Minister has every right to
ignore any advice given if he wishes.   Moreover it

is sometimes a matter of interpretation by the Minister as to what constitutes a matter of national interest. In its other role of appeal committee the Council's actions are similarly circumscribed by the fact that it can only deal with those cases that are referred to it from lower committees and such appeals might well be blocked by those groups in the lower committees that do not see it in their interests to have such an appeal made.

The Inspectors

Based in Paris, at the pinnacle of the multi-faceted French inspectorate, is the IGEN (Inspecteur général de l'Education nationale).(4) Though numbering only some 200, the IGEN possess considerable influence and prestige, enjoying direct access, usually through the head of the service, to the Minister of Education, the person by whom they are all appointed. In general terms, the IGEN is officially responsible for maintaining the standard and balance of the education system as a whole. He does this in a number of ways. Firstly, he is involved in the recruitment and training of teachers (who are employees of the state, not of local authorities). He oversees the various examinations which teachers must sit in order to qualify and, acting as chief examiner, he can chair the various assessment committees as well as take part in the actual examining of candidates. Secondly, he inspects qualified teachers, advising and giving impetus to in-service work. Thirdly, he devises the national syllabuses for the various subjects and levels of the education service from nursery school to lycée. Fourthly, he ensures the two-way flow of information from the centre of the system to the periphery. It can be appreciated that the IGEN is a key figure.

Each IGEN belonged to one of the following groups: French; foreign languages; pre-school, junior and special education; mathematics; physical sciences; natural sciences; industrial science and technique; technical education; philosophy; history and geography; social sciences; economy and management; artistic education; school organisation. The Minister of Education appoints a head of each group for two years and a chief inspector for five years. The chief inspector chooses certain IGEN to work as a committee with him which principally functions as a think-tank. A major responsibility of his is to ensure an exchange of information across group boundaries, the lack of communication often having been a cause of complaint in the past. Indeed this division into subject specialisms is reflected in schools, though the trend throughout the Fifth Republic has been to bring about greater cooperation between the groups of inspectors within the central administration. One example of this is the attendance at the meetings of other groups of those inspectors belonging to the school organisation group and that of the pre-school, junior and special education area. Representatives of the other sections also attend the meetings of these two groups.

These divisions within the central inspectorate date from the beginning of 1980(5) but it continues a process that received its first major impetus in 1960. By that date the Paris inspectorate had quietly evolved over the decades into over fifteen haphazard sections each with its own methods of recruitment and promotion and strictly limited to its own specialism. The idea of a general inspectorate had gradually been lost as individual inspectors were obliged to come into close contact with only those teachers whose specialism they shared. The reorganisation of the Ministry continued in the mid-sixties and made the inspectorate as a whole directly responsible to the Minister.(6)

The IGEN are men and women who have spent their lives moving up through the education service, first being teachers then inspectors and finally ending, like all top civil servants in France, in Paris. Moreover, they are in all probability among those who were the highest qualified in their profession. Although appointed by the Minister, they are chosen from a list drawn up by other IGEN. They are thus easy targets for the accusation that the corps is inward-looking and resistant to change. As a consequence, it has been argued, the IGEN has become of minor importance in an ever-moving education system. (7) There is some justification for these charges. The further one rises in a hierarchy the greater the likelihood of being out of touch with the grass roots (and the less likely that one will admit it). In October 1978 one inspector (a grade below an IGEN, therefore that much closer to the teachers) was asked if she thought the idea of mixed-ability classes (much debated at the time) had been called into question at all by any teachers. She replied: 'No; when you hear someone doing so it's only in jest. The principle of mixed-ability classes is not called into question by teachers'.(8) Need one add that it has been vehemently opposed by many teachers in France.(9)

However if it is sometimes said that the IGEN are out of touch, they are in a unique position to escape such a charge. They have responsibility for their subjects over large areas of the country and their areas are regularly changed. They are thus well-placed to obtain a reasonably complete picture of what is happening nationwide. Of course, it is possible for travel not only to broaden the mind but also to confirm prejudices. Nevertheless the IGEN have given plenty of evidence of their adaptability over the years, for example in the frequent modifications to the national syllabuses, and since they are often up-to-date with educational research (sometimes because they are involved in it) it is not unknown for them to be radical in their thinking.

That part of an IGEN's job (and that of all types of inspector) which causes the most controversy is the inspection of teachers and more particularly the awarding of a mark out of twenty for competence. The final mark is an amalgam of what the inspector awards for teaching ability and what the headmaster awards for administrative efficiency. It is important because it has a direct bearing upon the teacher's pay. A high mark can mean that he advances more rapidly through the pay scales. The idea behind such a system is of course that merit should be rewarded and in fact it was the teachers (in the post-war period) who asked for such a system to be instituted. The awarding of marks is not however the daunting prospect for a teacher that it first appears to be. The inspector has only a theoretical use of the full range from nought to twenty; for the overwhelming majority of teachers ten to fifteen is the range used. However there are virtually never any sudden departures from the last mark and such departures are rarely downwards. The expectation is that a teacher will start his career just over the halfway mark of the full scale (how could he have got through his training otherwise?) and as experience informs his practice so the mark rises. Often the worst that happens is that a teacher gets the same mark as his last inspection.

The inspector's visit is usually most unnerving for the new entrants to the profession since those with a certain amount of experience of such visits have a good idea of their own competence and what inspectors think of it. The old-fashioned tight-lipped inspection has in any case largely died out with inspectors more concerned to be helpers than judges. Teachers in general are less in awe and are more likely to speak their minds if an inspector

says something with which they do not agree. They
have been known for instance to tell an inspector
to come back on a day when the previous evening's
celebrations were not affecting their classroom
performance.

Inspections are not regularly carried out, nor
can they be, since the growth in teacher numbers
has not been matched by a similar growth in the
proportion of inspectors. It has become impossible
to inspect every teacher as frequently as they
theoretically should be. Inspectors therefore tend
to go and see entrants to the profession while it
is up to individuals among the remainder to put in a
formal request to be inspected. Some teachers have
not been inspected for five or even ten years.
Apart from the administrative difficulties involved,
there are several reasons for the criticism by some
teachers and most teachers' unions of this type of
mark-awarding inspection. Objections to the system
centre around the feeling that the process is de-
grading and rests upon criteria that are never made
explicit. Generally, teachers are mystified about
how either the administrative or the teaching mark
is arrived at. As a form of self-defence some
teachers have special lessons prepared in advance
(they usually receive notice of an inspector's
arrival). Moreover, the number of people who are to
benefit from higher rates of pay is fixed in advance
each year so even if a teacher imagines he has done
well during an inspection, he knows that any material
award is finally decided by what credits have been
allocated to his particular area for that year.

The result of all this has been a growing
tendency for a minority of teachers to refuse to be
inspected and the teachers' union SGEN in particular
has been prompt to support such actions. The issue
at stake is fundamentally the feasibility of someone
being both helper and judge. The inspector who
increasingly conceives his role as that of helper is
obviously hindered in his task if he is at the same
time the hierarchical superior. Some experts are of
the opinion that the dual role is impossible: 'You
cannot at the same time award marks to a teacher and
help him to look clearly at his problems. You cannot
encourage him, urge him to discover his own way if
you are seeking at the same time to judge him'.(10)

Opinions within the inspectorate vary on the
marking of teachers but some have for a long time
thought that little would be lost if this aspect of
their job were dropped. The fact that the IGEN does
not mark the performance of the head of a <u>collège</u>

171

or the administrative staff makes the relationship
with these that much easier.(11)   Perhaps the question is not whether it can or cannot be done since it
has been done.   Student-teachers are helped and
judged by various members of the teaching profession.
Perhaps the question should be whether or not it is
best done by the inspector.   Despite attacks upon
the system and a certain amount of evolution in the
inspector's role, all Ministers of Education to date
have answered in the affirmative.   The most recent
change has come with the arrival in power of the
socialist government in 1981.

The Socialist Government

The first socialist Minister of Education, Alain
Savary, wished to accentuate the cooperative nature
of education and all the early signs from Paris
indicated that reform on this basis was on the way.
It was no surprise therefore when the major report
on the secondary system, Pour un collège démocratique,(12) which was published in late 1982, gave an
impetus to such methods as team teaching in that
sector and suggested that the inspectorate should
place greater emphasis upon judging teachers as
members of a team rather than as individuals.   The
question was whether individual inspections should
cease altogether since unions close to the socialists,
such as SGEN, had repeatedly attacked this aspect of
the inspector's job.   The report addressed itself
to the problem of individual assessment within the
context of collective responsibility, declaring:

> Is it appropriate in these conditions to
> preserve individual evaluation of teachers?
> It is possible to imagine the disappearance
> of this latter function along with that of
> individual marking and promotion which are
> linked to it.   It has been emphasised, in
> fact, that it is difficult to evaluate people
> within a hierarchical system and to reply to
> their need for on-the-spot help.   This diffi-
> culty which is real is not insurmountable.(13)

Thus when Savary made public his deliberations
upon the IGEN in October 1982, he retained the contentious procedure of individual inspection including the marking of teachers.   However, he also laid
down how such inspections were to be carried out in
the future.   There should be a preliminary visit by
the inspector so that he could get to know the

school and the conditions in which it was operating and notice should be given of all visits as well as the reason for them. After each individual inspection a detailed discussion should take place with the teacher and his colleagues. The report (to which the teacher has a right of reply) would take into account the school situation and would be sent to the teacher within a month, though the marks would only be sent the following term after the appropriate committee had standardised all those for its particular area. If the mark was lower than the one received previously the teacher would have a right of appeal and could ask to be inspected again.

In this latest spirit of cooperation the groups of the IGEN were modified so that certain areas would be more closely associated. Thus French and modern languages were put together, as were mathematics, natural sciences and physical sciences; industrial sciences, technical education, economics and management, social sciences, history and geography, and philosophy. Artistic education and physical education remained as separate groups with the nursery, primary and special education group as well as that for school organisation continuing to take part as before in the work of the other groups.

There was nothing specifically socialist in all this since, as we have seen, the IGEN had been moving towards greater cooperation virtually from the outset of the Fifth Republic. The IGEN had also more recently become aware of the danger of isolation or at least appearing to be isolated, and a more open attitude on their part can be discerned in the 1980s. Whereas in 1979 the thought of allowing a journalist to accompany an IGEN into a classroom was anathema,(14) by 1983 this was considered a distinct possibility by the chief inspector.(15)

The role of the IGEN has been modified over the years though these inspectors do retain a considerable influence on what happens in the education service nationally. As we have seen, individual inspections are a good example of this for, whereas an IGEN can less easily act arrogantly, the mark he awards is still important. The role of the IGEN is as firmly a part of the French system as ever and this for important reasons. Many teachers support the idea of inspections. It is argued that if the individual marking of teachers were abolished then all would progress through the pay scales at a uniform rate (there being no separate scales for special responsibilities). There remains considerable opposition even among the teaching profession

to age being the major factor determining how well
individuals are paid. Most important of all however
the IGEN is seen as providing a degree of uniformity
and therefore fairness to the system. He is still
viewed as the guarantor of a national standard.
Local conditions may have their influence upon the
type of teaching in a certain school but the IGEN is
supposed to see everything in a wider context. He
therefore helps prevent idiosyncracies adulterating
good practice to a point where standards are eroded.
The national syllabuses ensure that at a time of
increased social mobility the most important element
in the system, the child, does not suffer if he goes
from one part of the country to another. Of course
national syllabuses drawn up by the IGEN cannot
guarantee equality of treatment but the French still
regard them as an important element in trying to
achieve it. So too the IGEN's oversight of teachers
on a national scale. The fears of the former
Giscardian Minister of Education, Christian Beullac,
that Savary's reforms would allow teachers themselves
to set their own standards because of the emphasis
on individuality, expressed those felt by many when
he wrote:

> For the teachers themselves the absence of an
> an exterior bench mark, of guidelines, of a
> mirror held up will be the source of anxiety
> and, finally, discouragement. Teachers cannot
> be a team playing without a referee, without
> spectators, without opponents, and without a
> ball, with nil as the score written up in
> advance.(16)

The Administrative Inspector

The other type of inspector based in Paris with
oversight of the national system, but on an even
wider scale than the IGEN, is the IGAEN (Inspecteur
général de l'administration de l'Education nationale). This category of inspector was created in
1965(17) by bringing together in one corps inspectors
who had been attached to a number of separate departments within the education system and who had
been responsible for their administration. The
IGAEN are now divided into three ranks: inspecteurs,
inspecteurs généraux adjoint and inspecteurs généraux. They number about 55 and the range of services,
departments and educational establishments which
they inspect is comprehensive since they cover the
whole of the state education system from nursery

schools to universities. The second article of the
decree establishing the IGAEN is often quoted to
illustrate the breadth of their responsibility:
'The members of this corps are responsible within
the administrative, financial, accounting and economic domain for the inspection of the personnel,
departments, establishments and, generally, of all
the organisations under the authority of the Ministry
of Education'. The IGAEN therefore cover the whole
of the non-teaching area of the French education
system. Because they are relatively few in number,
they tend to be reserved for the drawing up of
reports on large sectors of the service or on matters
affecting the whole of the education system. Examples
of studies carried out in recent years include one
on the structure and working of the Centre national
de la recherche scientifique, another on the Apprenticeship Centres and another on the means of implementing various educational reforms. The fact that
the IGAEN soon abandoned inspecting individuals has
meant that they have rarely come in for the sort of
criticism levelled at the IGEN. They are occasionally sent by the Minister to act as troubleshooters,
as for example in 1969 to the University of Vincennes
when the administration of the examinations had
temporarily broken down, but more usually they head
commissions and study groups looking into the many
aspects of the administration of the education service. Perhaps they have also attracted less criticism
because they have no power to enforce changes upon
an organisation upon which they have reported. That
power belongs either to the head of the particular
organisation or to the Minister of Education. In
this respect at least the IGAEN parallels the British
HMI since it is not rare for the advice from such
non-executive organs to be quietly ignored. However,
the IGAEN at least exercises an indirect influence
because his job consists of advising and training
administrative personnel, and the dissemination and
gathering of information - all of which are officially as important as inspecting.

The regional tier: the académie
The tier of educational organisation below that of
central government is based upon the académie.
This is a region which varies in size roughly
corresponding to population density and which is
usually based upon a large university town. Originally created by Napoleon and corresponding to areas
covered by the appeal courts, the académies were

175

changed in 1848 and again in 1854 when fourteen of
the list of sixteen were virtually the same as those
of today: Aix (now Aix-Marseille which includes the
island of Réunion), Besançon, Bordeaux, Caen, Cler-
mont, Dijon, Grenoble, Lyon, Montpellier, Nancy (now
Nancy-Metz), Poitiers, Rennes, Strasbourg and Toulouse. The Third Republic transferred the seat of
the fifteenth académie from Douai to Lille in 1888
whilst the sixteenth, Paris, had to wait for the
arrival of the Fifth Republic before it too was
altered. At the end of December 1971 Paris was
divided into three: Créteil, Versailles and the city
of Paris itself. The restructuring of the Paris
area was not the first time this century that a reorganisation of the académies had taken place, but
all major changes had been during the Fifth Republic.
The list had been radically altered in the sixties
by the creation of three académies in 1962: Nantes,
Orléans-Tours and Reims; two more in 1964: Amiens
and Rouen; and a further two in 1965: Limoges and
Nice. In the seventies (besides Paris) came the
académie des Antilles and de la Guyane(1973) and
Corsica(1975). The total is now twenty-seven.(18)
The number of départements in an académie can vary.
Thus Rouen, for example, consists of two (Eure and
Seine-Maritime) while Toulouse has eight (Ariège,
Aveyron, Gers, Haute-Garonne, Hautes-Pyrénées, Lot,
Tarn and Tarn-et-Garonne).

Presiding over the education service within an
académie is the Recteur. This post too was created
during the Napoleonic period. The Recteur represents the government in the provinces. This function
continues essentially today although aspects of the
role have of course changed. Because of various
alterations in the organisation of different parts
of government administration particularly in 1964 and
1972 the Recteur lost some of his financial independence to the regional Prefect. But despite the
inevitable ebb and flow of responsibility within the
French administrative system, the Recteur has on the
whole been given increased responsibilities under
the Fifth Republic. Before the war the Recteur was
really only of symbolic importance in the regions.
He could of course intervene when he saw fit but he
was supported only by a skeleton staff and therefore
was imperfectly informed about local educational
developments. It was the dramatic increase in the
school population during the Fifth Republic which
brought about a permanent change in his responsibilities as he attempted to cater for a swiftly
changing educational scene at the end of the fifties

and into the sixties. School building, for example, became a major programme as the government sought to accommodate the wave of new pupils. Gradually the number of people working within the rectorat grew until it now often contains a staff of hundreds.

Under the Fifth Republic the Recteur has changed in another equally important way. For about a century and a half after the creation of the post, it was expected that, once appointed, the holder would continue until retirement. Nowadays Recteurs change posts frequently either by being transferred to another académie or by quitting the job altogether. The change in the length of tenure was given its principal impetus by another factor however. Traditionally a Recteur was an apolitical animal whose role was simply to represent the government by ensuring the uniformity of application of the various government directives. Gradually however some Recteurs became involved in politics. In the seventies the majority who became thus involved were men of the Right. This is not surprising perhaps given that the Right enjoyed uninterrupted power in government for more than twenty years. The government thus did little to discourage the new trend and indeed sometimes encouraged it by, for example, transferring Recteurs to académies where they might most efficiently represent the Right in local politics. Recteurs also campaigned in general elections or actively supported other candidates. Two Recteurs, René Haby and Alice Saunier-Séité, were appointed to government posts during the presidency of Giscard.

The politicisation of the Recteur inevitably added to the instability of the function. Since each Recteur is appointed directly by the Minister of Education, his position is dependent upon the favour of that Minister (and perhaps other ministers in the government). Such favour has come to depend much more upon the political persuasions of the Recteur. Little wonder then that the accession of the Left to power in 1981 heralded dismissals among the Recteurs. Between 1981 and 1983 twenty-one of the twenty-seven French rectorats received new heads. It is true that not all those appointed were supporters of the Left(19) but such wholesale changes only reinforced the idea that the post is something of a temporary appointment. Not that the ex-Recteur would be thrown out on to the street. The single essential qualification for the post is that he should possess a doctorate and in practice this means that he is recruited from the ranks of teachers and administrators within the higher education sector, and he usually returns there.

With responsibility for such a diverse service within his region, the Recteur is, by virtue of his wide-ranging contacts, ideally placed to inform the Minister about what is happening locally as well as the various reactions to the government's conduct of the service. This information-gathering role is strengthened since officially all communications to Paris pass via the Recteur. Simultaneously he must pass down through the system - though he often appends comments of his own - information emanating from the Ministry. Although clearly depending greatly upon the Minister, the Recteur has been strengthened particularly under the Fifth Republic by many government initiatives to decentralise various powers. Besides being able to organise the rectorat more or less as he pleases, he can exercise considerable influence on the overall organisation of the whole education service in his area. He can determine the distribution of schools and catchment areas and he shares out the funds allocated to his académie. In addition he has general charge of the careers of those working for the education service. However if he can exercise pressure, he is also subject to it from various groups both within and without the service. Because of such pressures (exercised, for example, by teachers' unions), the Recteur, though nominally in a powerful position, cannot rule despotically (not at least if his career matters to him) but must take into account the strength of local feelings. He is thus often anxious to avoid - or at least lessen - conflict both between Paris and the académie and between groups within his region.

Since 1968 and the laws granting French universities greater independence, the powers of the Recteur in the higher education sector have been reduced. He is no longer for example the Président of all universities within his académie. Now universities elect their own Président. Nevertheless he still coordinates higher education studies within the académie and this task becomes particularly important when there is more than one university there.

Finally, it should perhaps be mentioned that the Recteur of the académie of Paris has two deputies: one who looks after the schools of the city, and the other the universities.

Apart from the various departments within the rectorat necessary to administer the education service, the Recteur depends upon various consultative committees and the regional inspectorate. Of

the consultative committees, the most important is
the Conseil académique which gives its opinions upon
the laws and circulars affecting the secondary
sector and presides over disciplinary hearings.
Historically this committee included the higher education sector in its brief but this has changed since
1968. However it was not until three years later
that university representation was lessened. The
growth in the higher education sector had added to
the imbalance of these committees and had led to the
over-representation of university members. Other
committees at this level include various commissions
administratives paritaires which have an equal
number of members representing the administration
(usually nominated by the Recteur) and of the various
categories of personnel appropriate to that committee.
These discuss conditions of service and thus teachers'
unions tend to play a major part in them. Such
committees often have their national equivalent.

Other categories of inspector
The organisation of the inspectorate at national
level is relatively simple but is less so within the
académie. Apart from the occasional changes in the
role of various inspectors or the creation of other
types of inspector for an experimental period, the
name of inspector is often given to a wide range of
jobs. For example, the medical inspector who has
overall charge of school medical services or the
inspector responsible for the distribution of information on the education system both regionally and
nationally are principally administrators rather
than inspectors as such. Certainly teachers are
unlikely to come into contact with such figures.
However the three other major categories of regional
inspector are better known to them: the IPR (Inspecteur pédagogique régional), the IPET (Inspecteur
principal de l'enseignement technique) and the IPJS
(Inspecteur principal de la jeunesse et des sports).
These are appointed by the Minister of Education from
applicants (at least in the case of the first two)
who must possess either a doctorate or an agrégation
and who have been vetted by inspectors already in
post.

The IPR is a subject specialist and is attached
to one of the subject categories of the IGEN. The
latter is his superior and may allocate him a special
responsibility within the académie. The IPET has a
specialism from the world of technical education and
the IPJS covers games and physical education. The

duties of these inspectors are considerable since
their ministry-given task is to ensure that the
teaching of their subject is of a high quality and
that it is efficiently organised.(20) They can even
sometimes be asked to take charge of their specialism
in more than one académie. This is especially true
of certain technical specialisms in which expertise
is relatively rare and which perhaps is taught in
only a handful of institutions.

These regional inspectors are involved in
teachers' careers from the beginning since they are
authorised to participate in and sometimes organise
initial training as well as in-service activities and
even adult education. They can have a say in the
appointment of teacher trainers. The inspector,
like the Recteur, ensures the two-way flow of information from the Ministry downwards and from those
working in the education service in the académie
upwards to the Ministry. Moreover he is supposed to
keep teachers informed about developments in the
académie and thus he must be told about any experiments or studies undertaken by schools.

The regional inspector is therefore pivotally
placed within the system and his authority is considerable. This tradition of authority tends (human
nature being what it is) to make the corps resist
anything it regards as a challenge to its status.
In the late sixties and early seventies mathematics
inspectors hindered rather than helped the independent institutes for the teaching of their subject,
the IREM (Instituts de recherches sur l'enseignement
des mathématiques) which were designed to provide in-
service education in mathematics so that teachers
could more easily cope with the latest developments
in the subject. The inspectors had always played a
preponderant role in teacher education and thus were
wary and critical of the new institutes - operating
as they did at the regional level - and largely
beyond their control.

The local tier: the département
The person in overall charge of the education
service within each département of the académie is
rather confusingly called the Inspecteur d'académie.
Although associated in the mind of the average
Frenchman almost exclusively with the primary sector,
the Inspecteur d'académie has wide powers in the
secondary sector as well.(21) He is the equivalent
in the département (apart from not having any
responsibility for the universities) of the Recteur

in the académie. His powers are fairly general
within the secondary sector: he can inspect all secondary schools and their financial and administrative arrangements. In addition he has oversight in
the matter of the baccalauréat examination and
appoints examiners for it. Nevertheless his power
is somewhat circumscribed in that most of those
working within the secondary sector are managed at a
national level. Moreover most secondary schools are
largely free to spend their allocation as they will
since they have enjoyed a certain financial independence following the introduction of the Haby law in
1975.

But if the Inspecteur d'académie has considerable powers in the secondary sector, his powers in
the primary sector are even wider. He can inspect
all the schools; he is head of all the inspectors
within the département channelling information to and
from them; he appoints teachers to particular schools
and is in charge of transfers between schools; he
appoints examiners and sometimes presides over the
various examination panels; he is intimately
involved in the training of primary school teachers
and in the construction of school buildings. The
position of the Inspecteur d'académie becomes a key
one when it is realised that in the primary sector
the administrative and inspecting functions are
closely tied in with primary teachers as a whole.
Whereas in the secondary sector different subject
specialists are linked only to their own specialist
inspectors (who are in any case less numerous as a
corps than those inspecting and administering the
primary sector) and are administered on a national
level, the primary sector is more tightly knit. The
Inspecteur d'académie is still widely regarded as
first and foremost the head of the primary school
teachers in a département.

To help him in his task he works closely with
several types of inspector who have their equivalent
at the regional level as well as a number of consultative committees. The Comité départemental de
l'enseignement technique promotes technical education
and is composed not only of inspectors and teachers
but representatives of commerce and industry. The
Conseil départemental de l'enseignement primaire
has a reasonable range of power which affects
primary education and so occasionally is rather more
than a consultative body. However such power tends
to be of minor interest to the primary school
teacher since 1972 when the responsibility for their
careers was transferred to the CAPD (Commission

administrative paritaire départementale). The CAPD
is composed of equal numbers of teachers and of
members of the administration.

At this third tier of the education system is
found the most numerous type of French education
inspector, the IDEN (Inspecteur départemental de
l'Education nationale) - a title given official
blessing only in 1972.(22) He has the right to
inspect any teacher in the primary, infant or nursery
sector, though in fact his role is not necessarily
confined to the schools in this sector. He might be
a specialist in remedial or special education or
indeed in a subject taught in secondary schools. In
the latter case, he would inspect the work of the
PEGC. It would be unusual however for him to inspect
the other types of teacher who might be working in a
collège, even if these taught the inspector's spec-
iality.

The awarding of marks to teachers and the drawing up of reports on their work is however only one
part of the job of an IDEN. What is striking about
the work of any inspector at the level of the département is the range of activities in which he is
involved, particularly as part of his job concerns
both the initial and in-service training of teachers.
Indeed it is the IDEN who organises the in-service
programme for the département. In France this
reflects, as already mentioned, the changing emphasis
in the role of the inspector since less importance
is attached to laying down the law to individual
teachers and more upon encouraging the teacher to
look critically at his own practices and to motivate
him to improve his methods. The authoritarian
inspector - though not dead - is increasingly rare.
Because he has been made more responsible in recent
years for staff development and for initial training,
he has been brought closer to teachers. This trend
has encouraged a more cooperative effort particularly at the level of the département. Once again the
IDEN is always informed, for example, of any new
work going on in any school. Indeed the Ministry of
Education insists that he be so.(23) In addition he
has many administrative duties. A selective list of
these would include: appointing part-time and temporary teachers; being involved in opening and closing
schools; the provision of school meals and transport;
giving advice on buildings; suggesting school holi-
day dates. In addition he has a major part in
liaison between the schools in his charge (he is
supposed to be responsible for some 350 teachers -
though numbers vary) and the various local authority

departments (it will be realised that the French
schools are largely independent of the local authorities) and all the other groups which have links
with schools.

The IDEN undergoes a training programme, candidates being drawn of course from the teaching profession. Generally speaking, there are three categories of men and women who are recruited. Firstly,
those who are over 26 years of age and have a degree
plus teaching qualification and a minimum of three
years' teaching experience; secondly, those who are
over 28 who hold the teaching qualification of a
PEGC and have at least five years' teaching experience; thirdly, those who are over 30 and are qualified to teach in the primary and nursery sector, and
who have taught for at least seven years. The
maximum age for entry into the inspectorate at the
level of the département is 45 - though in some
circumstances this may be higher.(24) Most IDEN
come from the first category - something which points
to the generally hierarchical nature of the education
system. This reliance upon certain academic qualifications for accession to the higher posts is reflected in addition in the qualifications demanded of
those who wish to become an IDEN from the third
category. A minimum certified educational standard
is demanded from all candidates roughly equivalent
to two years' study in higher education and if the
candidate does not possess this minimum, he or she
must sit an examination with the purpose of ascert-
aining his or her general level of education.(25)

It is of some interest to describe the process
through which the IDEN must pass. The written
examination consists of a five-hour paper which is
usually based upon documents of an educational
nature, and this is followed by an oral examination.
The candidate may choose to answer a question about
teaching within one of the categories: nursery education, primary education or a secondary sector
discipline. He is given an hour to prepare and then
fifteen minutes to deliver an exposé. This is then
followed by fifteen minutes of questions from the
examiners which seek to determine the candidate's
level of general knowledge as well as his knowledge
of the education service as a whole. The successful
candidates can look forward to two years' training
followed by a probationary year before being given a
permanent post. The trainee is first of all put
under the wing of an IDEN and involved in that
inspector's work as much as possible before being
given charge of about 50 teachers. He thus becomes

actively involved in initial and in-service training. At the end of the first year comes a formal
examination. The trainee must present and comment
upon a piece of work already done by him on the job
to the satisfaction of his examiners and he is then
questioned for forty-five minutes on it. The other
part of the examination consists of questions on the
legislation and organisation of the nursery, junior
and secondary sectors. The second year of the
course ends with a practical examination. The
trainee must carry out two inspections: one of a
junior or nursery class chosen for him (he must also
judge how well that class's work fits in with the
work of the school as a whole) and another of any
class which he may choose himself. In addition, he
must organise a short course of initial or in-service education and also present and assess one other
activity carried out during the year.(26) The in-
service aspect of the IDEN's work has become increasingly important over the years and especially since
1972. At that date primary school teachers were
awarded as part of their conditions of service the
right to the equivalent of one year's in-service
work to be taken over the whole of their career.
The Peretti Report estimates that each year 35,000
teachers should be undertaking courses totalling
six weeks.(27)

At the level of the département, the IDEN is
not responsible for the technical sector, this is
the domain of the IET (Inspecteur de l'enseignement
technique). The IET has the same conditions of
employment as the IDEN but in fact is something of
an anomaly in that he is responsible for overseeing
technical education beyond the boundaries of a
single département. Like his superior, the IPET,
he often has to cover a larger area if his specialism
is relatively uncommon. An IET's specialism would
not necessarily be strictly technical in nature. He
might be concerned with one of the following areas:
literary subjects (which could include a range of
arts subjects including modern languages); scientific subjects; commercial subjects; biology and applied
social sciences; industrial technical education;
art.(28) Thus an IET works particularly closely
with the staff of the technical lycées who teach
this range of subjects. His responsibilities and
training parallel those of the IDEN but with even
more emphasis on the liaison between schools and
various outside bodies, particularly professional,
commercial and industrial organisations.

The third type of inspector at this level is

the one who deals with sport and physical education. The IDJSL (<u>Inspecteur départemental de la jeunesse des sports et des loisirs</u>) reflects the institution- alised belief that this area of the curriculum is something apart because of its specialised nature. Again the work and training of the IDJSL parallels the other types of inspectors though he does not award marks to teachers. Because sporting activity is very strong outside school in France this type of inspector inevitably becomes involved in the sporting scene at many different levels and it is easy to understand that his is a very busy life.(29)

The final type of inspector at this level is the IIO (<u>Inspecteur de l'information et de l'organ- isation</u>). He coordinates all activity in the <u>centre d'information et d'orientation</u>. These centres dis- tribute information - paralleled by those at the regional and national level - usually directed at pupils and their parents, to do with option schemes within schools and the various qualifications and courses needed in order to pursue particular studies and training schemes in preparation for a job.

The French inspectorate therefore plays a central role in the education system. It is the backbone of the service running from the level of the <u>département</u> right through to the upper echelons of the Ministry of Education. The dual inspectorial and administrative role fixes it there firmly. The inspectorate is not just another part of the educat- ion service which can be easily ignored. The involv- ment in the initial and in-service training of teachers and the drawing up of nationally followed syllabuses mean that the inspectorate's presence in schools is real - more real to many teachers than that of the headmaster who has little responsibility for a school's curriculum. Not that the inspector's role, particularly as facilitator of a centralised system, is always appreciated but it is difficult to imagine how such a body of men and women, so intim- ately involved in the work of the service as a whole, could be radically altered without major repercussions for schools and educational administration. Certain- ly, the inspectorate's role is evolving but it seems set to keep its dominant position for the foresee- able future.

NOTES

1.   Décret du 28 juillet 1948
2.   Ministers of Education from the promulgation of the Constitution of the Fifth Republic (October 1958) to the time of writing (January 1985). The dates in brackets are when they were appointed.

Jean Berthoin (1.6.58)   André Boulloche (8.1.59)
Michel Debré (23.12.59)   Louis Joxe (15.1.60)
Pierre Guillaumat (23.11.60) Lucien Paye (20.1.61)
Pierre Sudreau (15.4.62)   Louis Joxe (14.10.62)
Christian Fouchet (7.12.62)   Alain Peyrefitte (8.4.67)
François-Xavier Ortoli (31.5.68) Edgar Faure (13.7.68)
Olivier Guichard (22.6.69)   Joseph Fontanet (6.7.72)
René Haby (29.5.74)   Christian Beullac (5.4.78)
Alain Savary (22.5.81) Jean-Pierre Chevènement
                                            (19.7.84)

3.   Le Monde de l'Education, oct.1983, p.21.
4.   Before 1980 the name was inspecteur général de l'instruction publique.
5.   See the Instruction of 4 January, 1980.
6.   Décret du 14 mars 1964.
7.   'tout porte à croire que l'Inspection Générale (...) n'a plus qu'un rôle marginal' Pascale Gruson, L'Etat enseignant, p.216.
8.   Le Courrier de l'Education, 16.10.78.
9.   For just one example see the editorial in Nouvelle Revue Pédagogique, mars 1979.
10.   Jacques Minot, L'Education nationale, p.152.
11.   See Jeanne Dejean in 'Inspection générale et animation', Cahiers Pédagogiques No.82, mai 1969, p.46.
12.   Louis Legrand, Pour un collège démocratique.
13.   Legrand, op.cit. p.129.
14.   See 'Les Inspecteurs contestés', L'Express, 22.3.80.
15.   See the interview given by Yves Martin in Cahiers de l'Education nationale, juin 1982.
16.   Le Monde, 11.2.83.
17.   Décret du 14 avril and modified by another on 13 March 1978.
18.   In 1970 vice-rectorats were created in the four French overseas territories of New Caledonia, French Polynesia, Saint-Pierre-et-Miquelon and the Wallis and Futura Islands.
19.   Even one of those dismissed by the new government was willing to concede this point. See 'Université: les recteurs recalés', L'Express, 22 jan.1982, p.31.

20. Circulaire du 24 juin, 1980.

21. The decree of 28 February 1947 (still in force) declared unambiguously: 'l'inspecteur d'académie est le directeur départementale de tous les services de l'Education nationale'.

22. Décret du 4 juillet 1972.

23. Décret du 4 juillet 1972.

24. The circular dated 7 April 1976 raises the maximum age for the following categories of people by the number of years they were engaged in national service; looking after children between the ages of nine and sixteen; looking after a handicapped person in the family. There is no age-limit for women obliged to work after the death of their husband.

25. This competitive examination consists of two parts. Firstly, a written paper lasting five hours usually based upon a text which calls for reflexion upon an educational issue. Secondly, there is an oral examination lasting half an hour, for fifteen minutes of which the candidate delivers an exposé on a matter relating to a sector of the education system of his choice; the remaining fifteen minutes are spent answering questions put to him by the panel on the education system as a whole.

26. Arrêté du 4 oct. 1979.

27. André de Peretti, La Formation des personnels de l'Education nationale, p.65.

28. Arrêté du 20 nov. 1973.

29. See René Guy, 'Les corps d'inspection: technique et jeunesse', Education, 10fév. 1977, p.4.

APPENDIX

The following are three examples of timetables for <u>baccalauréat</u> sections. The figures indicate the number of hours allocated to each subject per week.

Baccalauréat Al (Literature and mathematics)

	Yr 2	Yr 3
French	5	–
Philosophy	–	8
History-geography	4	4
Foreign language 1	3	3
Natural science	2	–
Physical science	$1\frac{1}{2}$	–
Physical education	2	2
Mathematics	5	5
Obligatory options	–	–

Baccalauréat C (Mathematics and Physical Science)

	Yr 2	Yr 3
French	4	–
Philosophy	–	3
History-geography	4	3
Foreign language	3	3
Mathematics	6	9
Physical science	5	5
Natural science	$2\frac{1}{2}$	2
Physical education	2	2
Obligatory options	–	–

189

Appendix

Baccalauréat de technicien F1 (Mechanics)

	Yr 2	Yr 3
French	3	-
Philosophy	-	2
History-geography	2	-
Foreign language	2	2
Physical science	3	4
Mathematics	4	$3\frac{1}{2}$
Technology theory	8	8
Technology practice	12	14

The information given in the tables above is taken from: Baccalauréat de l'enseignement du second degré: A1 Lettres et mathématiques. (Fiche ONISEP, déc.1983). Baccalauréat de l'enseignement du second degré: C Mathématiques et sciences physiques. (Fiche ONISEP, déc.1983). Baccalauréat de technicien. Construction mechanique BTn F1. (Fiche ONISEP, juillet 1983).

AFPA	Association pour la formation profess-ionnelle des adultes
ANPE	Agence nationale pour l'emploi
BEP	Brevet d'enseignement professionnel
BEPC	Brevet d'études du premier cycle
BT	Brevet de technicien
BTn	Baccalauréat de technicien
BTS	Brevet de technicien supérieur
CAMIF	Cooperative des adhérents de la mutuelle des instituteurs de France
CAP	Certificat d'aptitude professionnelle
CAP	Certificat d'aptitude pédagogique
CAPD	Commission administrative paritaire dép-artementale
CAPEPS	Certificat d'aptitude au professorat/professionnelle à l'enseignement physique et sportif
CAPES	Certificat d'aptitude au professorat/professionnelle à l'enseignement second-aire
CAPET	Certificat d'aptitude au professorat/professionnelle à l'enseignement tech-nique
CASDEN-BP	Caisse d'aide sociale de l'Education nationale - Banque Populaire
CCSD	Commission de circonscription du second degré
CDEP	Conseil départemental de l'enseignement primaire
CDET	Conseil départemental de l'enseignement technique
CDI	Centre de documentation et d'information
CE	Cours élémentaire
CEG	Collège d'enseignement général
CEP	Certificat d'éducation professionnelle
CES	Collège d'enseignement secondaire
CFA	Centre de formation d'apprentis
CFEN	Certificat de fin d'études normales
CM	Cours moyen
CNAL	Comité national d'action laïque
CNAM	Conservatoire des arts et des métiers
CNEC	Centre national d'enseignement par corr-espondance
CNESER	Conseil national de l'enseignement sup-érieur et de la recherche
CNRS	Centre national de la recherche scientif-

	ique
CP	Cours préparatoire
CPA	Classe préparatoire à l'apprentissage
CPGE	Classe préparatoire aux grandes écoles
CPPN	Classe pré-professionnelle de niveau
CPR	Centre pédagogique régional
CSEN	Conseil supérieur de l'Education nationale
CUIO	Cellule universitaire d'information et d'orientation
DDI	Diplôme de docteur ingénieur
DEA	Diplôme d'études approfondies
DESS	Diplôme d'études supérieures spécialisées
DEUG	Diplôme d'études universitaires générales
DEUST	Diplôme d'études universitaires scientifiques et techniques
EMT	Education manuelle et technique
ENA	Ecole nationale d'administration
ENNA	Ecole normale nationale d'apprentissage
ENS	Ecole normale supérieure
ESA	Ecole spéciale d'architecture
ESC	Ecole supérieure de commerce
ESCAE	Ecole supérieure de commerce et d'administration des entreprises
FEN	Fédération de l'Education nationale
HEC	Hautes études commerciales
IDEN	Inspecteur départemental de l'Education nationale
IDJSL	Inspecteur départemental de la jeunesse des sports et des loisirs
IGAEN	Inspecteur général de l'administration de l'Education nationale
IGEN	Inspecteur général de l'Education nationale
IIO	Inspecteur d'information et de l'orientation
INPG	Institut national polytechnique de Grenoble
INRP	Institut national de la recherche pédagogique (Before 1974 INRDP - Institut national de la recherche et de documentation pédagogique and before that the IPN or Institut Pédagogique National
INSA	Institut national des sciences appliquées
IPET	Inspecteur principal de l'enseignement technique
IPJSL	Inspecteur principal de la jeunesse des sports et des loisirs
IPN	See INRP
IPR	Inspecteur pédagogique regional
IREM	Institut de recherche sur l'enseignement

List of abbreviations

	des mathématiques
IUT	Institut universitaire de technologie
LEP	Lycée d'enseignement professionnel
LEPA	Lycee d'enseignement professionnel agricole
MAIF	Mutuelle assurances des instituteurs français
MEN	Ministère de l'Education Nationale
MGEN	Mutuelle générale de l'Education nationale
MIAGE	Maîtrise de méthodes informatiques appliquées à la gestion
MSG	Maîtrise de sciences et de gestion
MST	Maîtrise de sciences et techniques
ONISEP	Office national d'information sur les enseignements et les professions
PAE	Projet d'action éducative
PNE	Pactes nationaux pour l'emploi
PTCT	Professeur technique chef de travaux
RPR	Rassemblement pour la République
SES	Section d'éducation spécialisée
SGEN	Syndicat général de l'Education nationale
SIGES	Service de l'informatique de gestion et des statistiques (Before 1982 known as SEIS - Service des études informatiques et statistiques)
SNE-Sup	Syndicat national de l'enseignement supérieur
SNI-PEGC	Syndicat national des instituteurs-professeurs d'enseignement général de collège
Sup. de Co	(Ecole) supérieure de commerce
TUC	Travaux d'utilité collective
UER	Unité d'enseignement et de recherche
UFR	Unité de formation et de recherche
UNAPEL	Union nationale des associations de parents d'élèves de l'école libre
UNEF	Union nationale des étudiants français
UPA	Unité pédagogique d'architecture
ZEP	Zone d'éducation prioritaire

BIBLIOGRAPHY OF WORKS CONSULTED

Apart from the constantly revised collection of laws
and circulars covering the whole of the education
service, the Recueil des lois et règlements (in
which all circulars quoted can be found) plus articles from newspapers and journals as well as a
host of more ephemeral documents, I consulted the
following books which are usually mentioned in the
text or notes.

Ardagh, John. France in the Eighties. Penguin, 1982.
Baudelot, Christian and Establet, Roger. L'Ecole
primaire divise. Maspero, 1974.
Berger, Ida. Les instituteurs d'une génération à
l'autre. PUF, 1979.
Capelle, Jean. Tomorrow's Education: the French exper-
ience. Pergamon, 1967.
Coutty, Marc. Et le lycée, ça marche? Autrement No.
33, 1981.
Cherkaoui, Mohamed. Les Changements du système éduc-
atif en France 1950-80, PUF, 1982.
Crémieux-Brilhac. L'Education nationale. PUF, 1965.
Chevalier, Jacques. L'Enseignement supérieur. PUF,
1971.
David, M. and Lezine, I. Early Child Care in France.
Gordon and Breach, 1975.
Fraser, W.R. Reforms and Restraints in Modern French
Education. Routledge and Kegan Paul, 1971. Educat-
ion and Society in Modern France. 1963.
Géminard, Lucien. Le système scolaire: le collège au
centre des réformes. La Documentation Française, 1983.
Georges, G. et al. La Formation des maîtres. ESF,
1974.
Gruson, Pascale. L'Etat enseignant. Mouton-Ecole des
Hautes Etudes en Sciences Sociales, 1978.
Halls, W.D. Education, Culture and Politics in Mod-
ern France. Pergamon, 1976. Society, Schools and
Progress in France. Pergamon, 1965.
Laprévote, Gilles. La Formation des instituteurs
primaires dans les écoles normales (1881-1979): de la
cohérence à l'anomie. Thèse 3ᵉ cycle. Univ. Lyon, 1981.
Legrand, Louis. Pour une politique démocratique de
l'éducation. PUF, 1977. Pour un collège démocrat-
ique. La Documentation Française, 1982.
Magliulo, Bruno. Les Grandes écoles. PUF, 1982.
Majault, Joseph. L'Enseignement en France. McGraw-

194

Bibliography of Works Consulted

Hill, 1973.

Mialaret, Gaston. La Formation des enseignants. PUF, 1983.

Ministère de l'Education Nationale. L'Ecole maternelle. CNDP, 1980. Guide pratique de la scolarité. ONISEP, 1982. Repères et références statistiques sur les enseignements et la formation. SIGES, Edition 1984.

Minot, Jacques. L'Education nationale. Berger-Levrault, 1979. L'Entreprise Education nationale. Armand Colin, 1970.

Paty, Dominique. Douze collèges en France: enquête sur le fonctionnement des collèges publics aujourd'hui. La Documentation Française, 1981.

Peretti, André de. La Formation des personnels de l'Education nationale. La Documentation Française, 1982.

Prost, Antoine. L'Enseignement en France 1800-1967. Armand Colin, 1968. Les Lycées et leurs études au seuil du XXI siècle. Ministère de l'Education Nationale, 1983.

Schwartz, Laurent. Pour sauver l'université. Seuil, 1983.

Shinn, Jerry. L'Ecole polytechnique. Presses de la Fondation Nationale des Sciences Politiques, 1980.

SUDEL. Code Soleil, 1983.

Zimmermann, Daniel (ed). Questions-réponses sur le cours préparatoire. Les Editions ESF, 1975. Questions-réponses sur les cours élémentaires, 1976. Questions-réponses sur les cours moyens, 1976. Questions-réponses sur les collèges, 1980. Questions-réponses sur les lycées, 1979.

INDEX

d'éducation.
syllabus <u>see</u> Ministry of
    Education

tanning 105.
teachers 41, 45, 48, 52,
    53, 54, 62, 63, 86, 87,
    91, 109, 114, 143-61,
    164, 167, 168, 169, 170,
    172, 179, 181, 182
    agrégés 143, 152, 154-9,
    160 certifiés (CAPES)
    143, 152, 154-9, 160,
    chef de travaux 75 PEGC
    41, 55, 143, 144, 152-4,
    159, 182 primary 144-7,
    153, 159, 160 <u>see also</u>
    university.
team teaching 52, 53.
technical education 37, 45,
    52, 61, 63, 64, 76, 77-
    9, 106, 158-9, 173, 180,
    181, 184 pre-vocational
    classes 49, 51, 53, 63
    <u>see also</u> CPA, CPPN, IUT,
    <u>LEP, STS</u>.
technical drawing 63.
technology <u>see</u> science.
textiles 95, 105.
trade unions <u>see</u> unions.
translators 106.
travaux d'utilité collective
    96.

unemployment 94-6.
unions 43, 46, 48, 50, 54,
    57, 118, 127, 135, 139,
    144, 145, 167, 170, 178,
    FEN 145, SGEN 45, 171,
    172, SNE-Sup 127, SNI-
    PEGC 46, 145, UNEF 119.
unité d'enseignement et de
    recherche 121, 133.
    de formation et de rech-
    erche 133-4.
unité pédagogique d'arch-
    itecture 105.
university 99, 101, 107,
    110, 111, 113-27, 151,
    156, 178, <u>see also</u> IUT.

veterinary science 100,
    106.
vocational education
    <u>see</u> technical educ-
    ation.

writing 18-9, 21.

year groups (primary)
    15-6.
year repeating 2-3.

zone d'éducation prior-
    itaire 48, 49-50.